101 Favorite Cat Poems

CB

CONTEMPORARY
BOOKS
CHICAGO

Library of Congress Cataloging-in-Publication Data

101 Favorite cat poems.
    p.   cm.
    ISBN 0-8092-4078-5
    1. Cats—Poetry.   I. Title: One hundred and one
favorite cat poems.
PN6110.C3A14   1991
808.81'936—dc20
                                            90-49402
                                                CIP

In some cases it has been extremely difficult to trace the authors and publishers of poems. If, despite our honest endeavors, we have been guilty of neglect in acknowledging the copyright holder, we would appreciate notification so we may rectify the matter in subsequent printings.

This anthology was compiled by Sara L. Whittier.

Published by Contemporary Books, Inc.
180 North Michigan Avenue, Chicago, Illinois 60601
Manufactured in the United States of America
International Standard Book Number: 0-8092-4078-5

Acknowledgments

Thanks are due to many poets and their publishers and representatives for authorizing the use of the following poems.

"Cat" from *The Skin Spinners* by Joan Aiken, copyright © 1975 by Joan Aiken. Reprinted by permission of the publisher, Viking Penguin, a division of Penguin Books USA Inc.

"The Cat," "The Cat," and "Cats" by Charles Baudelaire from *Poems of Baudelaire: A Translation of Le Fleurs du Mal*, Roy Campbell, translator. Reprinted by permission of Collins Publishers.

"The Cat" by Ogden Nash, copyright © 1933 by Ogden Nash. Reprinted by permission of Curtis Brown Ltd.

"The Cat" by Lytton Strachey used with thanks to The Society of Authors as agents for the Strachey Trust.

"Cat!" copyright © 1938 by Eleanor Farjeon and renewed 1966 by Gervase Farjeon. "The Golden Cat" and "A Kitten" copyright © 1933, 1961 by Eleanor Farjeon. Reprinted by permission of HarperCollins Publishers.

"Catalog" by Rosalie Moore, copyright © 1940, 1968 by The New Yorker Magazine, Inc. Reprinted by permission.

"The Cat and an Old Rat," "The Cat and the Two Sparrows," and "The Cat Metamorphosed into a Woman" from *The Complete Fables of Jean de la Fontaine*, edited with a rhymed verse translation by Norman B. Spector, copyright © 1988 by Northwestern University Press. Reprinted by permission of Northwestern University Press.

"The Cat and the Moon" from *The Poems of W. B. Yeats: A New Edition*, edited by Richard J. Finneran, copyright © 1919 by Macmillan Publishing Company and renewed 1947 by Bertha Georgie Yeats. Reprinted by permission of Macmillan Publishing Company.

"Cat & the Weather" from *New & Selected Things Taking Place* by May Swenson, copyright © 1978 by May Swenson. Reprinted by permission of the Literary Estate of May Swenson.

"The Cat and the Wind" from *The Passages of Joy* by Thom Gunn, copyright © 1982 by Thom Gunn. Reprinted by permission of Farrar, Straus and Giroux, Inc., and by permission of Faber and Faber Ltd.

"Catnip and Dogwood" from *Tigers and Other Lilies* by Howard Moss, copyright © 1977 by Howard Moss. Reprinted by permission of Albert Stadler, executor, the Estate of Howard Moss.

"Cat's Meat" and "Milk for the Cat" from *Collected Poems* by Harold Monro, copyright © 1970 by Harold Monro. Reprinted by permission of Gerald Duckworth & Co. Ltd.

"The China Cat," "Five Eyes," "Puss," and "Supper" by Walter de la Mare reprinted by permission of The Literary Trustees of Walter de la Mare and The Society of Authors as their representative.

"Country Cat" and "On a Night of Snow" from *Night and the Cat* by Elizabeth Coatsworth, copyright © 1950 by Elizabeth Coats-

White Cats

PAUL VALERY
(1871–1945)

To Albert Dugrip

In the clear gold of sunlight, stretching their backs,
—White as snow—see the voluptuous cats,
Closing eyes jealous of their inner glooms,
Slumbering in the tepid warmth of their illumined
    fur.

Their coats have the dazzle of dawn-bathed glaciers.
Inside them, their bodies, frail, sinewy, and slender,
Feel the shiverings of a girl inside her dress,
And their beauty refines itself in endless languors.

No question but their Soul of old has animated
The flesh of a philosopher, or a woman's body,
For since then their dazzling and inestimable
    whiteness

Holding the mingled spendor of a grand premiere,
Ennobles them to a rank of calm contempt,
Indifferent to everything but *Light* itself!

Translated by David Paul

To My Cat

ROSAMUND MARRIOTT WATSON
(1863–1911)

Half loving-kindliness, and half disdain,
Thou comest to my call serenely suave,
With humming speech and gracious gestures grave,
In salutation courtly and urbane:
Yet must I humble me thy grace to gain—
For wiles may win thee, but no arts enslave,
And nowhere gladly thou abidest save
Where naught disturbs the concord of thy reign.
Sphinx of my quiet hearth! who deignst to dwell,
Friend of my toil, companion of mine ease,
Thine is the lore of Rā and Rameses;
That men forget dost thou remember well,
Beholden still in blinking reveries,
With sombre sea-green eyes inscrutable.

To a Cat

JOHN KEATS
(1795–1821)

Cat! who hast pass'd thy grand climacteric,
  How many mice and rats hast in thy days
  Destroy'd?—How many tit bits stolen? Gaze
With those bright languid segments green, and
    prick
Those velvet ears—but pr'ythee do not stick
  Thy latent talons in me—and upraise
  Thy gentle mew—and tell me all thy frays
Of fish and mice, and rats and tender chick.
Nay, look not down, nor lick thy dainty wrists—
  For all the wheezy asthma,—and for all
thy tail's tip is nick'd off—and though the fists
  Of many a maid have given thee many a maul,
Still is that fur as soft as when the lists
  In youth thou enter'dst on glass-bottled wall.

Pangur Bán

ANONYMOUS
(EIGHTH OR EARLY NINTH CENTURY)

I and Pangur Bán, my cat,
'Tis a like task we are at;
Hunting mice is his delight,
Hunting words I sit all night.

Better far than praise of men
'Tis to sit with book and pen;
Pangur bears me no ill will,
He too plies his simple skill.

'Tis a merry thing to see
At our tasks how glad are we,
When at home we sit and find
Entertainment to our mind.

Oftentimes a mouse will stray
In the hero Pangur's way;
Oftentimes my keen thought set
Takes a meaning in its net.

'Gainst the wall he sets his eye
Full and fierce and sharp and sly;
'Gainst the wall of knowledge I
All my little wisdom try.

When a mouse darts from its den
O how glad is Pangur then!
O what gladness do I prove
When I solve the doubts I love!

So in peace our tasks we ply,
Pangur Bán, my cat, and I;
In our arts we find our bliss,
I have mine and he has his.

Practice every day has made
Pangur perfect in his trade;
I get wisdom day and night
Turning darkness into light.

Translated by Robin Flower

Supper

WALTER DE LA MARE
(1873–1956)

Her pinched grey body,
In widow's fur,
Mousey daren't
From her wainscot stir;
Twitching nose,
And hollow ear,
She stoops and listens,
Stark with fear:
There, like a tiger,
Sleek and sly,
Grimalkin's crouched
With gloating eye,
Watching her door—
While over the crumbs
The dusk of deepening
Evening comes.

The Cat

CHARLES BAUDELAIRE
(1821–1867)

I

A fine strong gentle cat is prowling
As in his bedroom, in my brain;
So soft his voice, so smooth its strain,
That you can scarcely hear him miowling.

But should he venture to complain
Or scold, the voice is rich and deep:
And thus he manages to keep
The charm of his untroubled reign.

This voice, which seems to pearl and filter
Through my soul's inmost shady nook,
Fills me with poems, like a book,
And fortifies me, like a philtre.

His voice can cure the direst pain
And it contains the rarest raptures.
The deepest meanings, which it captures,
It needs no language to explain.

There is no bow that can so sweep
That perfect instrument, my heart:
Or make more sumptuous music start
From its most vibrant cord and deep,

Than can the voice of this strange elf,
This cat, bewitching and seraphic,
Subtly harmonious in his traffic
With all things else, and with himself.

II

So sweet a perfume seems to swim
Out of his fur both brown and bright,
I nearly was embalmed one night
From (only once) caressing him.

Familiar Lar of where I stay,
He rules, presides, inspires and teaches
All things to which his empire reaches.
Perhaps he is a god, or fay.

When to a cherished cat my gaze
Is magnet-drawn and then returns
Back to itself, it there discerns,
With strange excitement and amaze,

Deep down in my own self, the rays
Of living opals, torch-like gleams
And pallid fire of eyes, it seems,
That fixedly return my gaze.

Translated by Roy Campbell

The Cat

LYTTON STRACHEY
(1880–1932)

Dear creature by the fire a-purr,
    Strange idol eminently bland,
Miraculous puss! As o'er your fur
    I trail a negligible hand,

And gaze into your gazing eyes,
    And wonder in a demi-dream
What mystery it is that lies
    Behind those slits that glare and gleam,

And exquisite enchantment falls
    About the portals of my sense;
Meandering through enormous halls
    I breathe luxurious frankincense,

And ampler air, a warmer June
    Enfold me, and my wondering eye
Salutes a more imperial moon
    Throned in a more resplendent sky

Than ever knew this northern shore.
    O'strange! For you are with me too,
And I who am a cat once more
    Follow the woman that was you.

With tail erect and pompous march,
    The proudest puss that ever trod,
Through many a grove, 'neath many an arch,
    Impenetrable as a god,

Down many an alabaster flight
　　Of broad and cedar-shaded stairs,
While over us the elaborate night
　　Mysteriously gleams and glares!

Frightened Men

ROBERT GRAVES
(1895–1985)

We were not ever of their feline race,
Never had hidden claws so sharp as theirs
In any half-remembered incarnation;
Have only the least knowledge of their minds
Through a grace on their part in thinking aloud;
And we remain mouse-quiet when they begin
Suddenly in their unpredictable way
To weave an allegory of their lives,
Making each point by walking round it—
Then off again, as interest is warmed.
What have they said? Or unsaid? What?
We understood the general drift only.

They are punctilious as implacable,
Most neighbourly to those who love them least.
A shout will scare them. When they spring, they
　　seize.
The worst is when they hide from us and change
To something altogether other:
We meet them at the door, as who returns
After a one-hour-seeming century
To a house not his own.

The Cat and the Wind

THOM GUNN
(b. 1929)

A small wind
blows across the hedge
into the yard.
The cat cocks her ears
—multitudinous rustling
and crackling all around—
her pupils dwindle
to specks in
her yellow eyes
that stare first upward
and then on every side
unable to single out
any one thing
to pounce on,
for all together
as if orchestrated,
twigs, leaves,
small pebbles, pause
and start and pause
in their shifting,
their rubbing
against each other.

She is still listening
when the wind is already
three gardens off.

To Winky

AMY LOWELL
(1874–1925)

Cat,
Cat,
What are you?
Son, through a thousand generations, of the black
    leopards
Padding among the sprigs of young bamboo;
Descendant of many removals from the white
    panthers
Who crouch by night under the loquat-trees?
You crouch under the orange begonias,
And your eyes are green
With the violence of murder,
Or half-closed and stealthy
Like your sheathed claws.
Slowly, slowly,
You rise and stretch
In a glossiness of beautiful curves,
Of muscles fluctuating under black, glazed hair.

Cat,
You are a strange creature.
You sit on your haunches
And yawn,
But when you leap
I can almost hear the whine
Of a released string,
And I look to see its flaccid shaking
In the place whence you sprang.

You carry your tail as a banner,
Slowly it passes my chair,
But when I look for you, you are on the table
Moving easily among the most delicate porcelains.
Your food is a matter of importance
And you are insistant on having
Your wants attended to,
And yet you will eat a bird and its feathers
Apparently without injury.

In the night, I hear you crying,
But if I try to find you
There are only the shadows of rhododendron leaves
Brushing the ground.
When you come in out of the rain,
All wet and with your tail full of burrs,
You fawn upon me in coils and subtleties;
But once you are dry
You leave me with a gesture of inconceivable
        impudence,
Conveyed by the vanishing quirk of your tail
As you slide through the open door.

You walk as a king scorning his subjects;
You flirt with me as a concubine in robes of silk.
Cat,
I am afraid of your poisonous beauty,
I have seen you torturing a mouse.
Yet when you lie purring in my lap
I forget everything but how soft you are,
And it is only when I feel your claws open upon
        my hand
That I remember—

Remember a puma lying out on a branch above my
    head
Years ago.

Shall I choke you, Cat,
Or kiss you?
Really I do not know.

She Sights a Bird

EMILY DICKINSON
(1830–1886)

She sights a Bird—she chuckles—
She flattens—then she crawls—
She runs without the look of feet—
Her eyes increase to Balls—

Her Jaws stir—twitching—hungry—
Her Teeth can hardly stand—
She leaps, but Robin leaped the first—
Ah, Pussy, of the Sand,

The Hopes so juicy ripening—
You almost bathed your Tongue—
When Bliss disclosed a hundred Toes—
And fled with every one—

Peter

MARIANNE MOORE
(1887–1972)

Strong and slippery,
built for the midnight grass-party
confronted by four cats, he sleeps his time away—
the detached first claw on the foreleg corresponding
to the thumb, retracted to its tip; the small tuft of
      fronds
or katydid-legs above each eye numbering all units
in each group; the shadbones regularly set about
      the mouth
to droop or rise in unison like porcupine-quills.
He lets himself be flattened out by gravity,
as seaweed is tamed and weakened by the sun,
compelled when extended, to lie stationary.
Sleep is the result of his delusion that one must
do as well as one can for oneself,
sleep—epitome of what is to him the end of life.
Demonstrate on him how the lady placed a forked
      stick
on the innocuous neck-sides of the dangerous
      southern snake.
One need not try to stir him up; his prune-shaped
      head
and alligator-eyes are not party to the joke.
Lifted and handled, he may be dangled like an eel
or set up on the forearm like a mouse;
his eyes bisected by pupils of a pin's width,
are flickeringly exhibited, then covered up.
May be? I should have said might have been;
when he has been got the better of in a dream—
as in a fight with nature or with cats, we all know it.

Profound sleep is not with him a fixed illusion.
Springing about with froglike accuracy, with jerky
     cries
when taken in hand, he is himself again;
to sit caged by the rungs of a domestic chair
would be unprofitable—human. What is the good
     of hypocrisy?
It is permissable to choose one's employment,
to abandon the nail, or roly-poly,
when it shows signs of being no longer a pleasure,
to score the nearby magazine with a double line of
     strokes.
He can talk but insolently says nothing. What of it?
When one is frank, one's very presence is a
     compliment.
It is clear that he can see the virtue of naturalness,
that he does not regard the published fact as a
     surrender.
As for the disposition invariably to affront,
an animal with claws should have an opportunity
     to use them.
The eel-like extension of trunk into tail is not an
     accident.
To leap, to lengthen out, divide the air, to purloin,
     to pursue.
To tell the hen: fly over the fence, go in the wrong
     way
in your perturbation—this is life;
to do less would be nothing but dishonesty.

Poem

WILLIAM CARLOS WILLIAMS
(1833–1963)

As the cat
climbed over
the top of

the jamcloset
first the right
forefoot

carefully
then the hind
stepped down

into the pit of
the empty
flowerpot

Haikat

MYRNA DAVIS
(b. 1936)

Suddenly head in air
staring intently
at no thing I can see

My Cat Major

Stevie Smith
(1902–1971)

Major is a fine cat
What is he at?
He hunts birds in the hydrangea
And in the tree
Major was ever a ranger
He ranges where no one can see.

Sometimes he goes up to the attic
With a hooped back
His paws hit the iron rungs
Of the ladder in a quick kick
How can this be done?
It is a knack.

Oh Major is a fine cat
He walks cleverly
And what is he at, my fine cat?
No one can see.

Catalog

ROSALIE MOORE
(b. 1910)

Cats sleep fat and walk thin.
Cats, when they sleep, slump;
When they wake, pull in—
And where the plump's been
There's skin.
Cats walk thin.

Cats wait in a lump.
Jump in a streak.
Cats, when they jump, are sleek
As a grape slipping its skin—
They have technique.
Oh, cats don't creak.
They sneak.

Cats sleep fat.
They spread comfort beneath them
Like a good mat,
As if they picked the place
And then sat.
You walk around one
As if he were the City Hall
After that.

If male,
A cat is apt to sing upon a major scale:
This concert is for everybody, this
Is wholesale.
For a baton, he wields a tail.

(He is also found,
When happy, to resound
With an enclosed and private sound.)

A cat condenses.
He pulls in his tail to go under bridges,
And himself to go under fences.
Cats fit
In any size box or kit;
And if a large pumpkin grew under one,
He could arch over it.

When everyone else is just ready to go out,
The cat is just ready to come in.
He's not where he's been.
Cats sleep fat and walk thin.

The Retired Cat

WILLIAM COWPER
(1731–1800)

A Poet's Cat, sedate and grave
As poet well could wish to have,
Was much addicted to inquire
For nooks to which she might retire,
And where, secure as mouse in chink,
She might repose, or sit and think.
I know not where she caught the trick—
Nature perhaps herself had cast her
In such a mould PHILOSOPHIQUE,
Or else she learn'd it of her Master.
Sometimes ascending, debonnair,
An apple-tree, or lofty pear,
Lodg'd with convenience in the fork,
She watch'd the gard'ner at his work;
Sometimes her ease and solace sought
In an old empty wat'ring-pot,
There wanting nothing, save a fan,
To seem some nymph in her sedan
Apparell'd in exactest sort,
And ready to be borne to court.

But love of change it seems has place
Not only in our wiser race,
Cats also feel, as well as we,
That passion's force, and so did she.
Her climbing, she began to find,
Expos'd her too much to the wind,
And the old utensil of tin
Was cold and comfortless within:

She therefore wish'd instead of those
Some place of more serene repose,
Where neither cold might come, nor air
Too rudely wanton with her hair,
And sought it in the likeliest mode
Within her master's snug abode.

A draw'r, it chanc'd, at bottom lined
With linen of the softest kind,
With such as merchants introduce
From India, for the ladies' use,
A draw'r impending o'er the rest,
Half open in the topmost chest,
Of depth enough, and none to spare,
Invited her to slumber there;
Puss with delight beyond expression
Survey'd the scene and took possession.
Recumbent at her ease ere long,
And lull'd by her own humdrum song,
She left the cares of life behind,
And slept as she would sleep her last,
When in came, housewifely inclined,
The chambermaid, and shut it fast,
By no malignity impell'd,
But all unconscious whom it held.

Awaken'd by the shock, (cried Puss)
'Was ever cat attended thus!
'The open draw'r was left, I see,
'Merely to prove a nest for me,
'For soon as I was well composed
'Then came the maid, and it was closed.
'How smooth these 'kerchiefs and how sweet!
'Oh what a delicate retreat!

21

'I will resign myself to rest
'Till Sol declining in the west
'Shall call to supper, when, no doubt,
'Susan will come and let me out.'

   The evening came, the sun descended,
And puss remain'd still unattended.
The night roll'd tardily away,
(With her indeed 'twas never day)
The sprightly morn her course renew'd,
The evening grey again ensued,
And puss came into mind no more
Than if entomb'd the day before.
With hunger pinch'd, and pinch'd for room,
She now presaged approaching doom,
Nor slept a single wink or purr'd,
Conscious of jeopardy incurr'd.

That night, by chance, the poet watching,
Heard an inexplicable scratching;
His noble heart went pit-a-pat,
And to himself he said—'What's that?'
He drew the curtain at his side,
And forth he peep'd, but nothing spied;
Yet, by his ear directed, guess'd
Something imprison'd in the chest,
And, doubtful what, with prudent care
Resolv'd it should continue there.
At length, a voice which well he knew,
A long and melancholy mew,
Saluting his poetic ears,
Consoled him, and dispell'd his fears;

He left his bed, he trod the floor,
He 'gan in haste the draw'rs explore,
The lowest first, and without stop
The rest in order to the top.
For 'tis a truth well known to most,
That whatsoever thing is lost,
We seek it, ere it come to light,
In ev'ry cranny but the right.
Forth skipp'd the cat, not now replete
As erst with airy self-conceit,
Nor in her own fond apprehension
A theme for all the world's attention,
But modest, sober, cur'd of all
Her notions hyperbolical,
And wishing for a place of rest
Any thing rather than a chest.
Then stepp'd the poet into bed.
With this reflection into his head.

MORAL

Beware of too sublime a sense
Of your own worth and consequence.
The man who dreams himself so great,
And his importance of such weight,
That all around in all that's done
Must move and act for Him alone,
Will learn in school of tribulation
The folly of his expectation.

Hodge, the Cat

SARAH CHAUNCY WOOLSEY
(SUSAN COOLIDGE)
(1835?–1905)

Burly and big, his books among,
   Good Samuel Johnson sat,
With frowning brows and wig askew,
His snuff-strewn waistcoat far from new;
So stern and menacing his air,
   That neither Black Sam, nor the maid
To knock or interrupt him dare;
   Yet close beside him, unafraid,
      Sat Hodge, the cat.

"This participle," the Doctor wrote,
   "The modern scholar cavils at,
But,"—even as he penned the word,
A soft, protesting note was heard;
The Doctor fumbled with his pen,
   The dawning thought took wings and flew,
The sound repeated, come again,
   It was a faint, reminding "Mew!"
      From Hodge, the cat.

"Poor Pussy!" said the learned man,
   Giving the glossy fur a pat,
"It is your dinner time, I know,
And—well, perhaps I ought to go;
For if Sam every day were sent
   Off from his work your fish to buy,
Why, men are men, he might resent,
   And starve or kick you on the sly;
      Eh! Hodge, my cat?"

The Dictionary was laid down,
　　The Doctor tied his vast cravat,
And down the buzzing street he strode,
Taking an often-trodden road,
And halted at a well-known stall:
　　"Fishmonger," spoke the Doctor gruff,
"Give me six oysters, that is all;
　　Hodge knows when he has had enough,
　　　　Hodge is my cat."

Then home; puss dined, and while in sleep
　　He chased a visionary rat,
His master sat him down again,
Rewrote his page, renibbed his pen;
Each "i" was dotted, each "t" was crossed,
　　He labored on for all to read,
Nor deemed that time was waste or lost
　　Spent in supplying the small need
　　　　Of Hodge, the cat.

The dear old Doctor! fierce of mien,
　　Untidy, arbitrary, fat,
What gentle thought his name enfold!
So generous of his scanty gold.
So quick to love, so hot to scorn,
　　Kind to all sufferers under heaven,
A tend'rer despot ne'er was born;
　　His big heart held a corner, even
　　　　For Hodge, the cat.

Puss

WALTER DE LA MARE
(1873–1956)

Puss loves man's winter fire
Now that the sun so soon
Leaves the hours cold it warmed
In burning June.

She purrs full length before
The heaped-up hissing blaze,
Drowsy in slumber down
Her head she lays.

While he with whom she dwells
Sits snug in his inglenook,
Stretches his legs to the flames
And reads his book.

The Stray Cat

EVE MERRIAM
(b. 1916)

It's just an old alley cat
that has followed us all the way home.

It hasn't a star on its forehead,
or a silky satiny coat.

No proud tiger stripes, no dainty tread,
no elegant velvet throat.

It's a splotchy, blotchy
city cat, not a pretty cat,
a rough little tough little bag of old bones.

"Beauty," we shall call you.
"Beauty, come in."

From *Ruth Pitter on Cats*

RUTH PITTER
(b. 1897)

The British poet Ruth Pitter dedicated an entire book of verse to the subject of cats. In the following two poems she depicts two young cats that are down, but far from out.

Mister the Blitzkit

For K.

Double, double, toil and trouble,
Crumps and bumps and lumps of rubble,
Little Mister, six weeks old,
Hungry, frightened, dirty, cold,
Has no mother, home, nor dinner,
But he's sharp for a beginner.
From his crevice he surveys
Those who walk the ruined ways;
From their faces he can tell
Who would treat a kitten well.
The big policeman, good but gruff—
Let him pass; he's rather rough,
And as a conscientious man
Might pop him in a certain Van.

A kindly matron comes to view.
She's nice—but what about the stew?
When her four fat kids have done
There's not much left for anyone.
Beside, those kids would give him hell.
Let her go, then. Wait a spell.
Here's a warden; that's a frost—
He's got no home except his post.
Soldier, sailor—damn, no good.
Cripes, he could down a bit of food.
And O hell, here comes the rain.
Stick it, Mister, try again.

Ah, here she comes, the very one!
The fact is obvious as the sun.
Young as he is, now Mister knows
He can bid farewell to woes.
In her countenance he reads
That she will satisfy his needs.
Food, fire, bed—he ticks them off—
Worm-dose, mixture for his cough,
Velvet mouse for when he plays,
Brush and comb, and holidays
In the countryside afar,
Or boarded out with loving char.
She will pick him up correctly
And always touch him circumspectly,
Like a really first-class mother
Never neglect, yet never bother.
The greatest wonder is that he
Knows that there is a vacancy,
Which has allowed a thieving band
Of mice to get the upper hand.

Forth he darts—with piteous grace
Looks up mewing in her face.
Six weeks old—but what a grip
On the art of salesmanship!
Youth, dirt, fear, all play their part
In the lady's feeling heart.
A word of love, a mutual kiss,
And he is hers, and she is his.
Because he is so small and weak
She holds him closely to her cheek,
Takes him home, through wind and rain,
And will not let him go again.

Arrived, he finds he did not err
In his estimate of her.
Warm milk, a nice old woollen vest,
And he soon sinks to blissful rest.
When he awakes, his coat will be
Brushed into strict propriety,
And in the evening she will seal
Their love with a substantial meal,
And let him lay his clever head
Close to her own warm heart, in bed.

Three Cheers for the Black, White and Blue

Johnny is a long-haired Blue,
Looks a gentleman to you.
But his Ma was black and white,
Loved a dustbin, loved a fight;
And her little orphan boy,
Dressed up à la Fauntleroy,
Brushed and combed to look the part,
Has a wicked alley heart;
Swipes a titbit, smites a foe
With a fierce and expert blow;
Hands a deadly sock to those
Who interfere with his repose;
Circles round, intent to slog,
Any inoffensive dog;
Is profuse in phrases terse
And turns a ready, witty curse.
Yet he's a taking little brute,
The Bruiser in his ritzy suit.

The Kitten and Falling Leaves

WILLIAM WORDSWORTH
(1770–1850)

That way look, my Infant, lo!
What a pretty baby-show!
See the Kitten on the wall,
Sporting with the leaves that fall,
Withered leaves—one—two—and three—
From the lofty elder-tree!
Through the calm and frosty air
Of this morning bright and fair,
Eddying round and round they sink
Softly, slowly: one might think,
From the motions that are made,
Every little leaf conveyed
Sylph or Faery hither tending,—
To this lower world descending,
Each invisible and mute,
In his wavering parachute.
——But the Kitten, how she starts,
Crouches, stretches, paws, and darts!
First at one, and then its fellow
Just as light and just as yellow;
There are many now—now one—
Now they stop and there are none.
What intenseness of desire
In her upward eye of fire!
With a tiger-leap half-way
Now she meets the coming prey,
Lets it go as fast, and then
Has it in her power again:

Now she works with three or four,
Like an Indian conjurer;
Quick as he in feats of art,
Far beyond in joy of heart.
Were her antics played in the eye
Of a thousand standers-by,
Clapping hands with shout and stare,
What would little Tabby care
For the plaudits of the crowd?
Over happy to be proud,
Over wealthy in the treasure
Of her own exceeding pleasure!
　　'Tis a pretty baby-treat;
Now, I deem, for me unmeet;
Here, for neither Babe nor me,
Other play-mate can I see.
Of the countless living things,
That with stir of feet and wings
(In the sun or under shade,
Upon bough or grassy blade)
And with busy revellings,
Chirp and song, and murmurings,
Made this orchard's narrow space,
And this vale so blithe a place;
Multitudes are swept away
Never more to breathe the day:
Some are sleeping; some in bands
Travelled into distant lands;
Others slunk to moor and wood,
Far from human neighbourhood;
And, among the Kinds that keep
With us closer fellowship,
With us openly abide,
All have laid their mirth aside.

Where is he that giddy Sprite,
Blue-cap, with his colours bright,
Who was blest as bird could be,
Feeding in the apple-tree;
Made such wanton spoil and rout,
Turning blossoms inside out;
Hung—head pointing towards the ground—
Fluttered, perched, into a round
Bound himself, and then unbound;
Lithest, gaudiest Harlequin!
Prettiest Tumbler ever seen!
Light of heart and light of limb;
What is now become of Him?
Lambs, that through the mountains went
Frisking, bleating merriment
When the year was in its prime,
They are sobered by this time.
If you look to vale or hill,
If you listen, all is still,
Save a little neighbouring rill,
That from out the rocky ground
Strikes a solitary sound.
Vainly glitter hill and plain,
And the air is calm in vain;
Vainly Morning spreads the lure
Of a sky serene and pure;
Creature none can she decoy
Into open sign of joy:
Is it that they have a fear
Of the dreary season near?
Or that other pleasures be
Sweeter even than gaiety?

Yet, whate'er enjoyments dwell
In the impenetrable cell
Of the silent heart which Nature
Furnishes to every creature;
Whatsoe'er we feel and know
Too sedate for outward show,
Such a light of gladness breaks,
Pretty Kitten! from thy freaks,—
Spreads with such a living grace
O'er my little Dora's face;
Yes, the sight so stirs and charms
Thee, Baby, laughing in my arms,
That almost I could repine
That your transports are not mine,
That I do not wholly fare
Even as ye do, thoughtless pair!
And I will have my careless season
Spite of melancholy reason,
Will walk through life in such a way
That, when time brings on decay,
Now and then I may possess
Hours of perfect gladsomeness.
—Pleased by any random toy;
By a kitten's busy joy,
Or an infant's laughing eye
Sharing in the ecstasy;
I would fare like that or this,
Find my wisdom in my bliss;
Keep the sprightly soul awake,
And have faculties to take,
Even from things by sorrow wrought,
Matter for a jocund thought,
Spite of care, and spite of grief,
To gambol with Life's falling Leaf.

A Kitten

ELEANOR FARJEON
(1881–1965)

He's nothing much but fur
And two round eyes of blue,
He has a giant purr
And a midget mew.

He darts and pats the air,
He starts and cocks his ear,
When there is nothing there
For him to see and hear.

He runs around in rings,
But why we cannot tell;
With sideways leaps he springs
At things invisible—

Then half-way through a leap
His startled eyeballs close,
And he drops off to sleep
With one paw on his nose.

Confidence

MARTHA BAIRD
(1921–1981)

Little cats walk with their tails up.
Happy, they are afraid of nothing.
They will hiss at a big dog or a big person,
Not to defend themselves,
But to show their spirit.

Familiarity Dangerous

WILLIAM COWPER
(1731–1800)

As in her ancient mistress' lap,
   The youthful tabby lay,
They gave each other many a tap,
   Alike dispos'd to play.

But strife ensues. Puss waxes warm,
   And with protruded claws
Ploughs all the length of Lydia's arm,
   Mere wantonness the cause.

At once, resentful of the deed,
   She shakes her to the ground
With many a threat, that she shall bleed
   With still a deeper wound.

But, Lydia, bid thy fury rest!
   It was a venial stroke;
For she, that will with kittens jest,
   Should bear a kitten's joke.

(Translated from a Latin poem by Vincent Bourne)

The Kitten

JOANNA BAILLIE
(1762–1851)

Wanton droll, whose harmless play
Beguiles the rustic's closing day,
When, drawn the evening fire about,
Sit aged crone and thoughtless lout,
And child upon his three-foot stool,
Waiting until his supper cool,
And maid, whose cheek outblooms the rose,
As bright the blazing faggot glows,
Who bending to the friendly light,
Plies her task with busy sleight;
Come, show thy tricks and sportive graces,
Thus circled round with merry faces!

Backward coil'd and crouching low,
With glaring eyeballs watch thy foe,
The housewife's spindle whirling round,
Or thread, or straw, that on the ground
Its shadow throws, by urchin sly
Held out to lure thy roving eye;
Then stealing onward, fiercely spring
Upon the tempting, faithless thing.
Now, whirling round with bootless skill,
Thy bo-peep tail provokes thee still,
As still beyond thy curving side
Its jetty tip is seen to glide;
Till from thy centre starting far,
Thou sidelong veer'st with rump in air
Erected stiff, and gait awry,
Like madam in her tantrums high;

Though ne-er a madam of them all,
Whose silken kirtle sweeps the hall,
More varied trick and whim displays
To catch the admiring stranger's gaze.

Doth power in measured verses dwell,
All thy vagaries wild to tell?
Ah no! the start, the jet, the bound,
The giddy scamper round and round,
With leap and toss and high curvet,
And many a whirling somerset
(Permitted by the modern Muse
Expression technical to use),
These mock the deftest rhymester's skill,
But poor in art, though rich in will,
The featest tumbler, stage bedight,
To thee is but a clumsy wight,
Who every limb and sinew strains
To do what costs thee little pains;
For which, I trow, the gaping crowd
Requites him oft with plaudits loud.
But, stopp'd the while thy wanton play,
Applauses too thy pains repay:
For then beneath some urchin's hand
With modest pride thou tak'st thy stand,
While many a stroke of kindness glides
Along thy back and tabby sides.
Dilated swells thy glossy fur,
And loudly croons thy busy purr,
As, timing well the equal sound,
Thy clutching feet bepat the ground,
And all their harmless claws disclose
Like prickles of an early rose,
While softly from thy whisker'd cheek
Thy half-closed eyes peer, mild and meek.

But not alone by cottage fire
Do rustics rude thy feats admire.
The learnd sage, whose thoughts explore
The widest range of human lore,
Or with unfetter'd fancy fly
Through airy heights of poesy,
Pausing, smiles with alter'd air
To see thee climb his elbow-chair,
Or, struggling on the mat below,
Hold welfare with his slipper'd toe.
The widow'd dame, or lonely maid,
Who, in the still, but cheerless shade
Of home unsocial, spends her age,
And rarely turns a letter'd page,
Upon her hearth for thee lets fall
The rounded cork or paper ball,
Nor chides thee on thy wicked watch,
The ends of ravell'd skein to catch,
But lets thee have thy wayward will,
Perplexing oft her better skill.

E'en he, whose mind of gloomy bent,
In lonely tower, or prison pent,
Reviews the coil of former days,
And loathes the world and all its ways;
What time the lamp's unsteady gleam
Hath roused him from his moody dream,
Feels, as thou gambol'st round his seat,
His heart of pride less fiercely beat,
And smiles, a link in thee to find,
That joins it still to living kind.

Whence hast thou then, thou witless puss,
The magic power to charm us thus?
Is it that in thy glaring eye
And rapid movements, we descry—
Whilst we at ease, secure from ill,
The chimney corner snugly fill—
A lion darting on his prey,
A tiger at his ruthless play?
Or, is it, that in thee we trace
With all thy varied wanton grace,
An emblem, view'd with kindred eye,
Of tricky, restless infancy?
Ah! many a lightly sportive child,
Who hath like thee our wits beguiled,
To dull and sober manhood grown,
With strange recoil our hearts disown.
Even so, poor kit! must thou endure,
When thou become'st a cat demure,
Full many a cuff and angry word,
Chid roughly from the tempting board,
And yet, for that thou hast, I ween,
So oft our favoured playmate been,
Soft be the change, which thou shalt prove,
When time hath spoiled thee of our love;
Still be thou deem'd, by housewife fat,
A comely, careful, mousing cat,
Whose dish is, for the public good,
Replenish'd oft with savoury food.
Nor, when thy span of life be past,
Be thou to pond or dunghill cast;
But gently borne on goodman's spade,
Beneath the decent sod be laid,
And children show, with glistening eyes,
The place where poor old Pussy lies.

Ode to a Bob-Tailed Cat

ANONYMOUS

Felis Infelix! Cat unfortunate,
    With nary narrative!
Canst thou no tail relate
      Of how
      (Miaow!)
Thy tail end came to terminate
      So bluntly?
Didst wear it off by
      Sedentary habits
      As do the rabbits?

Didst go a
      Fishing with it,
      Wishing with it
      To "bob" for catfish,
And get bobbed thyself?
      Curses on that fish!

Didst lose it in kittenhood,
      Hungrily chawing it?
Or, gaily pursuing it,
      Did it make tangent
From thy swift circuit?

Did some brother Grayback—
      Yowling
      And howling
In nocturnal strife,
      Spitting and staring,
      Cursing and swearing,

Ripping and tearing,
  Calling thee "Sausagetail,"
Abbreviate thy suffix?

Or did thy jealous wife
  Detect yer
In some sly flirtation,
  And, after caudal lecture,
Bite off thy termination?
And sarve yer right!

Did some mischievous boy,
  Some barbarous boy,
  Eliminate thy finis?
  (Probably!)
  The wretch!
  The villain!
  Cruelly spillin'
  Thy innocent blood!

  Furiously scratch him
Where'er yer may catch him!

Well, Bob, this course now is left,
Since thus of your tail you're bereft:
  Tell your friend that by letter
  From Paris
You have learned the style there is
  To wear the tail short,
  And the briefer the better;
  Such is the passion,
That every Grimalkin will
  Follow your fashion.

Cat's Meat

HAROLD MONRO
(1879–1932)

Ho, all you cats in all the street;
Look out, it is the hour of meat:

The little barrow is crawling along,
And the meat-boy growling his fleshy song.

Hurry, Ginger! Hurry, White!
Don't delay to court or fight.

Wandering Tabby, vagrant Black,
Yamble from adventure back!

Slip across the shining street,
Meat! Meat! Meat! Meat!

Lift your tail and dip your feet;
Find your penny—Meat! Meat!

Where's your mistress? Learn to purr;
Pennies emanate from her.

Be to her, for she is Fate,
Perfectly affectionate.

(You, domestic Pinkie-Nose,
Keep inside, and warm your toes.)

Flurry, flurry in the street—
Meat! Meat! Meat! Meat!

Cat

JOAN AIKEN
(b. 1924)

Old Mog comes in and sits on the newspaper
Old fat sociable cat
Thinks when we stroke him he's doing us a favour
Maybe he's right, at that.

The Kitten

OGDEN NASH
(1902–1971)

The trouble with a kitten is
THAT
Eventually it becomes a
CAT.

From *The Golden Gate*

VIKRAM SETH
(b. 1952)

*A cat is a key character in Vikram Seth's novel in verse,
The Golden Gate. Here are three passages on the fear-
some tabby named Charlemagne.*

Why scratch a scratching post when trousers
Present themselves? Why bite a bone?
Why hunt mere mice like lesser mousers
When, having gnawed the telephone
Receiver when you sensed the presage
Of an impending urgent message
From John's curt boss, who can't afford
To waste time, you can short the cord?
Why vex yourself with paltry matters
When a report named *Bipartite
Para-Models of Missile Flight*
Can casually be torn to tatters?
And why, in short, crave vapid food
When you can drink your foe's heart's
        blood?

Blood! This is no farfetched analogy.
In this connection it's germane
To note his psychic genealogy:
The warrior blood of Charlemagne
Brims with—a bonus for a rhymer—
The hunting spirit of Selima,
The wits of Fritz, the fierce élan
Of the exultant Pangur Bán.
The grand Tiberian Atossa
And the electric Cat Jeoffry
Are honored in a pedigree
Long as your arm and high as Ossa.
I list these but to illustrate
The hybrid vigor of the great.

. . . .

What did that purr reflect? The tender
Fealty of a one-person cat?
Or memories of nights of splendor
When with a snarling caveat
The territorial marauder
Scattered his rivals in disorder
To quench some she-cat's arching wiles
Upon the clattering star-lit tiles?
Or, as he aged, the sweet security
Of love that mellows in old casks
Whose ebbing essence molds and masks
The vintage of its youthful purity?—
Old Cat, who with the injured roar
Of lions, once more paws the door!

Cat!

ELEANOR FARJEON
(1881–1965)

Cat!
Scat!
Atter her, atter her,
Sleeky flatterer,
Spitfire chatterer,
Scatter her, scatter her
Off her mat!
Wuff!
Wuff!
Treat her rough!
Git her, git her,
Whiskery spitter!
Catch her, catch her,
Green-eyed scratcher!
Slathery
Slithery
Hisser,
Don't miss her!
Run till you're dithery,
Hithery,
Thithery!
Pfitts! pfitts!
How she spits!
Spitch! spatch!
Can't she scratch!

Scritching the bark
of the sycamore-tree,
She's reached her ark
And's hissing at me
     Pfitts! pfitts!
     Wuff! wuff!
     Scat,
     Cat!
     That's
     That!

Pussycat Sits on a Chair

EDWARD NEWMAN HORN
(1903?–1976)

Pussycat sits on a chair
Implacably with acid stare.

Those who early loved in vain
Use the cat to try again,

And test their bruised omnipotence
Against the cat's austere defense.

The Singing Cat

STEVIE SMITH
(1902–1971)

It was a little captive cat
    Upon a crowded train
His mistress takes him from his box
    To ease his fretful pain.

She holds him tight upon her knee
    The graceful animal
And all the people look at him
    He is so beautiful.

But oh he pricks and oh he prods
    And turns upon her knee
Then lifteth up his innocent voice
    In plaintive melody.

He lifteth up his innocent voice
    He lifteth up, he singeth
And to each human countenance
    A smile of grace he bringeth.

He lifteth up his innocent paw
    Upon her breast he clingeth
And everybody cries, Behold
    The cat, the cat that singeth.

He lifteth up his innocent voice
    He lifteth up, he singeth
And all the people warm themselves
    In the love his beauty bringeth.

Woman and Cat

PAUL VERLAINE
(1844–1896)

She was playing with her cat,
and it was marvelous to see
white hand and white paw, pitty-pat,
spar in the evening sportively.

The little wretch hid in her paws,
those black silk mittens, murderously,
the deadly agate of her claws,
keen as a razor's edge can be.

Her steel drawn in, the other seemed
all sugar, the sly hypocrite,
but the devil didn't lose a bit . . .

and in the room where, sonorous,
her airy laughter rang, there gleamed
four sharp points of phosphorous.

Translated by C. F. MacIntyre

Esther's Tomcat

TED HUGHES
(b. 1930)

Daylong this tomcat lies stretched flat
As an old rough mat, no mouth and no eyes,
Continual wars and wives are what
Have tattered his ears and battered his head.

Like a bundle of old rope and iron
Sleeps till blue dusk. Then reappear
His eyes, green as ringstones: he yawns wide red,
Fangs fine as a lady's needle and bright.

A tomcat sprang at a mounted knight,
Locked round his neck like a trap of hooks
While the knight rode fighting its clawing and bite.
After hundreds of years the stain's there

On the stone where he fell, dead of the tom:
That was at Barnborough. The tomcat still
Grallochs odd dogs on the quiet,
Will take the head clean off your simple pullet,

Is unkillable. From the dog's fury,
From gunshot fired point-blank he brings
His skin whole, and whole
From owlish moons of bekittenings

Among ashcans. He leaps and lightly
Walks upon sleep, his mind on the moon.
Nightly over the round world of men,
Over the roofs go his eyes and outcry.

The China Cat

WALTER DE LA MARE
(1873–1956)

You never stir, and heaven forbid,
Since, mutest companion, if you did—
A creature formed of clay and glaze—
Nature herself would stand at gaze,
Albeit it with an intent to flatter:
Man would have conjured life from matter—
If from your bowels there should befall
A low protracted caterwaul,
Those slanting eyes should open and pause,
Those pads eject their hidden claws.
No nightlong vigil I know well
Would consummate that miracle;
Yet even that passive attitude
Once did a questing dog delude.

Lays of Tom-cat Hiddigeigei

J. V. SCHEFFEL
(1826–1886)

I

When through valley and o'er mountain
Howls the storm at dead of night,
Clambering over roof and chimney,
Hiddigeigei seeks the height;

Spectre-like aloft he stands there,
Fairer than he ever seems;
From his eyes the fire-flame sparkles,
From his bristling hair it streams.

And he lifts his voice, and wildly
Sings an old cat-battle song,
That, like far-off thunder rolling,
Sweeps the storm-vexed night along.

Never a child of man can hear it—
Each sleeps heedless in his house;
But, deep down in darkest cellar,
Hears, and paling, quakes the mouse.

Well she knows the greybeard's war-cry,
Knows the cry she trembles at,
Feels how fearful in his fury
Is the grand old hero-cat.

II

From the tower's topmost angle
On the world I turn my eyes—
Mark, serene, the factions wrangle,
And the parties fall and rise.

And the keen cat's eyes they see there—
And the cat's soul feels the joke—
What dull pranks they cut beneath there,
All those petty pigmy-folk.

But what use? For I can't make 'em
See things from my point of view;
Even should the devil take 'em,
'Twill but be the devil's due.

Human nature! who can bear it?
Crooked ways and wicked wiles!
Wrapt in consciousness of merit,
Sits the tom-cat on the tiles!

Translated by William Fitzgerald

Lisy's Parting with Her Cat

JAMES THOMSON
(1700–1748)

The dreadful hour with leaden pace approached,
Lashed fiercely on by unrelenting fate,
When Lisy and her bosom Cat must part:
For now, to school and pensive needle doomed,
She's banished from her childhood's undashed joy,
And all the pleasing intercourse she kept
With her grey comrade, which has often soothed
Her tender moments while the world around
Glowed with ambition, business, and vice,
Or lay dissolved in sleep's delicious arms;
And from their dewy orbs the conscious stars
Shed on their friendship influence benign.

But see where mournful Puss, advancing, stood
With outstretched tail, casts looks of anxious woe
On melting Lisy, in whose eyes the tear
Stood tremulous and thus would fain have said,
If Nature had not tied her struggling tongue:
"Unkind, O! who shall now with fattening milk,
With flesh, with bread, and fish beloved, and meat,
Regale my taste? and at the cheerful fire,
Ah, who shall bask me in their downy lap?
Who shall invite me to the bed, and throw
The bedclothes o'er me in the winter night,
When Eurus roars? Beneath whose soothing hand
Soft shall I purr? But now, when Lisy's gone,
What is the dull officious world to me?
I loathe the thoughts of life:" Thus plained the cat,
While Lisy felt, by sympathetic touch,
These anxious thoughts that in her mind revolved,

And casting on her a desponding look,
She snatched her in her arms with eager grief,
And mewing, thus began: "O Cat beloved!
Thou dear companion of my tender years!
Joy of my youth! that oft has licked my hands
With velvet tongue ne'er stained by mouse's blood.
Oh, gentle Cat! how shall I part with thee?
How dead and heavy will the moments pass
When you are not in my delighted eye,
With Cubi playing, or your flying tail.
How harshly will the softest muslin feel,
And all the silk of schools, while I no more
Have your sleek skin to soothe my softened sense?
How shall I eat while you are not beside
To share the bit? How shall I ever sleep
While I no more your lulling murmers hear?
Yet we must part—so rigid fate decrees—
But never shall your loved idea dear
Part from my soul, and when I first can mark
The embroidered figure on the snowy lawn,
Your image shall my needle keen employ.
Hark! now I'm called away! O direful sound!
I come—I come, but first I charge you all—
You—you—and you, particularly you,
O, Mary, Mary, feed her with the best,
Repose her nightly in the warmest couch,
And be a Lisy to her!"—Having said,
She set her down, and with her head across,
Rushed to the evil which she could not shun,
While a sad mew went knelling to her heart!

The Talking Family

RUTH PITTER
(b. 1897)

With the early morning tea
   Start the day's debates.
Soon the Talking Family
   Gathers, gravitates
To the largest room and bed,
That all may share in what is said.

All the Cats forgather too,
   With a calm delight,
Tab and ginger, long-haired blue,
   Seem to think it right
That they should share to some extent
In this early parliament.

Perhaps they only want a drink
   (Which of course they get)
But myself I like to think
   That the Cats are met
Because this animal rejoices
In the sound of human voices.

What they are we do not know,
   Nor what they may become.
Perhaps the thoughts that ebb and flow
   In a human home
May blow to brightness the small spark
They carry through the vasty dark.[1]

[1]Perque pruinosas tulit *irrequieta* tenebras.—Ovid.

On a Cat Aging

ALEXANDER GRAY
(1882–1968)

He blinks upon the hearth-rug
And yawns in deep content,
Accepting all the comforts
That Providence has sent.

Louder he purrs, and louder,
In one glad hymm of praise,
For all the night's adventures,
For quiet, restful days.

Life will go on for ever,
With all that cat can wish;
Warmth, and the glad procession
Of fish, and milk and fish.

Only—the thought disturbs
        him—
He's noticed once or twice,
The times are somehow breeding
A nimbler race of mice.

Milk for the Cat

HAROLD MONRO
(1879–1932)

When the tea is brought at five o'clock,
And all the neat curtains are drawn with care,
The little black cat with bright green eyes
Is suddenly purring there.

At first she pretends, having nothing to do,
She has come in merely to blink by the grate,
But though tea may be late or the milk may be
    sour,
She is never late.

And presently her agate eyes
Take a soft large milky haze,
And her independent casual glance
Becomes a stiff, hard gaze.

Then she stamps her claws or lifts her ears
Or twists her tail and begins to stir,
Till suddenly all her lithe body becomes
One breathing, trembling purr.

The children eat and wriggle and laugh;
The two old ladies stroke their silk:
But the cat is grown small and thin with desire,
Transformed to a creeping lust for milk.

The white saucer like some full moon descends
At last from the cloud of the table above;
She sighs and dreams and thrills and glows,
Transfigured with love.

She nestles over the shining rim,
Buries her chin in the creamy sea;
Her tail hangs loose; each drowsy paw
Is doubled under each bending knee.

A long dim ecstasy holds her life;
Her world is an infinite shapeless white,
Till her tongue has curled the last holy drop
Then she sinks back into the night,

Draws and dips her body to heap
Her sleepy nerves in the great arm-chair,
Lies defeated and buried deep
Three or four hours unconscious there.

Gray Thrums

CLARA DOTY BATES
(1838–1895)

Which is the cosiest voice,
The piping droning noise
      When the kettle hums,
Or this little old-fashioned wheel
      Spinning gray thrums?

Gray thrums! what wheel, you ask,
Turns at such pleasant task
      With a soft whirr?
Why, the one in pussy's throat
      That makes her purr.

Listen the rippling sound,
And think how round and round
      The spindle goes,
As the drowsy thread she spins
      Drowsily grows.

What will she do with it
When it is finished? Knit
      Some mittens new?
Or shuttle it, and weave cloth
      As weavers do?

A funny idea that,
A spinning wheel in a cat!
      Yet how it hums!
Our puss is gray, so of course
      She spins gray thrums.

Lullaby for the Cat

Elizabeth Bishop
(1911–1979)

Minnow, go to sleep and dream,
   Close your great big eyes;
Round your bed Events prepare
   The pleasantest surprise.

Darling Minnow, drop that frown,
   Just cooperate,
Not a kitten shall be drowned
In the Marxist State.

Joy and Love will both be yours,
   Minnow, don't be glum.
Happy days are coming soon—
   Sleep, and let them come . . .

Cat & the Weather

MAY SWENSON
(b. 1919)

Cat takes a look at the weather.
Snow.
Puts a paw on the sill.
His perch is piled, is a pillow.

Shape of his pad appears.
Will it dig? No.
Not like sand.
Like his fur almost.

But licked, not liked.
Too cold.
Insects are flying, fainting down.
He'll try

to bat one against the pane.
They have no body and no buzz.
And now his feet are wet;
it's a puzzle.

Shakes each leg,
then shakes his skin
to get the white flies off.
Looks for his tail,

tells it to come on in
by the radiator.
World's turned queer
somehow. All white,

no smell. Well, here
inside it's still familiar.
He'll go to sleep until
it puts itself right.

Fog

CARL SANDBURG
(1878–1967)

The fog comes
on little cat feet.

It sits looking
over harbor and city
on silent haunches
and then moves on.

December Cats

MARK VAN DOREN
(1894–1972)

Less and less they walk the wild
Cold world of dark, of windy snow.
Curiosity comes in;
There is nothing more to know;
Examines corners; yawns and dies,
Warm under lamps and buzzing flies.

The oldest beast, with panther head,
The latest yielded: ran in tracks
Himself had punctured; hid by stones,
And pounced, and crackled mice's backs.
But now that all midwinter wests,
Even he the ranger rests.

That Cat

BEN KING
(1857–1894)

The cat that comes to my window sill
When the moon looks cold and the night is still—
He comes in a frenzied state alone
With a tail that stands like a pine tree cone,
And says: "I have finished my evening lark,
And I think I can hear a hound dog bark.
My whiskers are froze'nd stuck to my chin.
I do wish you'd git up and let me in."
      That cat gits in.

But if in the solitude of the night
He doesn't appear to be feeling right,
And rises and stretches and seeks the floor,
And some remote corner he would explore,
And doesn't feel satisfied just because
There's no good spot for to sharpen his claws,
And meows and canters uneasy about
Beyond the least shadow of any doubt
      That cat gits out.

On a Night of Snow

ELIZABETH COATSWORTH
(1893–1986)

Cat, if you go outdoors you must walk in the
    snow.
You will come back with little white shoes on your
    feet,
Little white slippers of snow that have heels of
    sleet.
Stay by the fire, my Cat. Lie still, do not go.
See how the flames are leaping and hissing low,
I will bring you a saucer of milk like a marguerite,
So white and so smooth, so spherical and so
    sweet—
Stay with me, Cat. Outdoors the wild winds blow.

Outdoors the wild winds blow, Mistress, and dark
    is the night.
Strange voices cry in the trees, intoning strange
    lore;
And more than cats move, lit by our eyes' green
    light
On silent feet where the meadow grasses hang
    hoar—
Mistress, there are portents abroad of magic and
    might,
And things that are yet to be done. Open the door!

The Cat and the Moon

WILLIAM BUTLER YEATS
(1865–1939)

The cat went here and there
And the moon spun round like a top,
And the nearest kin of the moon,
The creeping cat, looked up.
Black Minnaloushe stared at the moon,
For, wander and wail as he would,
The pure cold light in the sky
Troubled his animal blood.
Minnaloushe runs in the grass
Lifting his delicate feet.
Do you dance, Minnaloushe, do you dance?
When two close kindred meet,
What better than call a dance?
Maybe the moon may learn,
Tired of that courtly fashion,
A new dance turn.
Minnaloushe creeps through the grass
From moonlit place to place,
The sacred moon overhead
Has taken a new phase.
Does Minnaloushe know that his pupils
Will pass from change to change,
And that from round to crescent,
From crescent to round they range?
Minnaloushe creeps through the grass
Alone, important and wise,
And lifts to the changing moon
His changing eyes.

The Song of the Jellicles

T. S. ELIOT
(1888–1965)

Jellicle Cats come out to-night,
Jellicle Cats come one come all:
The Jellicle Moon is shining bright—
Jellicles come to the Jellicle Ball.

Jellicle Cats are black and white,
Jellicle Cats are rather small;
Jellicle Cats are merry and bright,
And pleasant to hear when they caterwaul.
Jellicle Cats have cheerful faces,
Jellicle Cats have bright black eyes;
They like to practise their airs and graces
And wait for the Jellicle Moon to rise.

Jellicle Cats develop slowly,
Jellicle Cats are not too big;
Jellicle Cats are roly-poly,
They know how to dance a gavotte and a jig.
Until the Jellicle Moon appears
They make their toilette and take their repose:
Jellicles wash behind their ears,
Jellicles dry between their toes.

Jellicle Cats are white and black,
Jellicle Cats are of moderate size;
Jellicles jump like a jumping-jack,
Jellicle Cats have moonlit eyes.

They're quiet enough in the morning hours,
They're quiet enough in the afternoon,
Reserving their terpsichorean powers
To dance by the light of the Jellicle Moon.

Jellicle Cats are black and white,
Jellicle Cats (as I said) are small;
If it happens to be a stormy night
They will practise a caper or two in the hall.
If it happens the sun is shining bright
You would say they had nothing to do at all:
They are resting and saving themselves to be right
For the Jellicle Moon and the Jellicle Ball.

The King of Cats Sends a Postcard to His Wife

NANCY WILLARD
(b. 1936)

Keep your whiskers crisp and clean.
Do not let the mice grow lean.
Do not let yourself grow fat
like a common kitchen cat.

Have you set the kittens free?
Do they sometimes ask for me?
Is our catnip growing tall?
Did you patch the garden wall?

Clouds are gentle walls that hide
gardens on the other side.
Tell the tabby cats I take
all my meals with William Blake,

lunch at noon and tea at four,
served in splendor on the shore
at the tinkling of a bell.
Tell them I am sleeping well.

Tell them I have come so far,
brought by Blake's celestial car,
buffeted by wind and rain,
I may not get home again.

Take this message to my friends.
Say the King of Catnip sends
to the cat who winds his clocks
a thousand sunsets in a box,

to the cat who brings the ice
the shadows of a dozen mice
(serve them with assorted dips
and eat them like potato chips),

and to the cat who guards his door
a net for catching stars, and more
(if with patience he abide):
catnip from the other side.

The Mysterious Cat

VACHEL LINDSAY
(1879–1931)

I saw a proud, mysterious cat,
I saw a proud, mysterious cat,
Too proud to catch a mouse or rat—
Mew, mew, mew.

But catnip she would eat, and purr,
But catnip she would eat, and purr,
And goldfish she did much prefer—
Mew, mew, mew.

I saw a cat—'twas but a dream,
I saw a cat—'twas but a dream,
Who scorned the slave that brought her cream—
Mew, mew, mew.

Unless the slave were dressed in style,
Unless the slave were dressed in style,
And knelt before her all the while—
Mew, mew, mew.

Did you ever hear of a thing like that?
Did you ever hear of a thing like that?
Did you ever hear of a thing like that?
Oh, what a proud mysterious cat.
Oh, what a proud mysterious cat.
Oh, what a proud mysterious cat.
Mew . . . mew . . . mew.

A Cat's Conscience

ANONYMOUS

A dog will often steal a bone,
But conscience lets him not alone,
And by his tail his guilt is known.

But cats consider theft a game,
And, howsoever you may blame,
Refuse the slightest sign of shame.

When food mysteriously goes,
The chances are that Pussy knows
More than she leads you to suppose.

And hence there is no need for you,
If Puss declines a meal or two,
To feel her pulse and make ado.

The Owl and the Pussy-cat

Edward Lear
(1812–1888)

The Owl and the Pussy-cat went to sea
  In a beautiful pea-green boat,
They took some honey, and plenty of money,
  Wrapped up in a five-pound note.
The Owl looked up to the stars above,
  And sang to a small guitar,
'O lovely Pussy! O Pussy, my love,
  What a beautiful Pussy you are,
      You are,
      You are!
  What a beautiful Pussy you are!'

Pussy said to the Owl, 'You elegant fowl!
  How charmingly sweet you sing!
O let us be married! too long have we tarried:
  But what shall we do for a ring?'
They sailed away, for a year and a day,
  To the land where the Bong-tree grows,
And there in a wood a Piggy-wig stood
  With a ring at the end of his nose,
      His nose,
      His nose,
  With a ring at the end of his nose.

'Dear Pig, are you willing to sell for one shilling
  Your ring?' Said the Piggy, 'I will.'
So they took it away, and were married next day
  By the Turkey who lives on the hill.

They dined on mince, and slices of quince,
   Which they ate with a runcible spoon;
And hand in hand, on the edge of the sand,
   They danced by the light of the moon,
      The moon,
      The moon,
   They danced by the light of the moon.

Catnip and Dogwood

HOWARD MOSS
(1922–1987)

A cat's quite different from a dog
And you name it differently, too;
A library cat might be Catalogue,
And a Siamese, Fu Manchu.
Dogs usually have humdrum names
Like Molly, Blacky, Biff, and James.

Cats eat catnip excitedly,
Get drunk and jump around,
But a dog can sniff at a dogwood tree,
And sniff and sniff quite diligently,
Sit down and never budge—
And be as smug and sober as a judge.

From *The Cat in the Hat*

THEODOR SEUSS GEISEL (DR. SEUSS)
(b. 1904)

The sun did not shine.
It was too wet to play.
So we sat in the house
All that cold, cold, wet day.

I sat there with Sally.
We sat there, we two.
And I said, "How I wish
We had something to do!"

Too wet to go out
And too cold to play ball.
So we sat in the house.
We did nothing at all.

So all we could do was to
Sit!
    Sit!
        Sit!
            Sit!
And we did not like it.
Not one little bit.

And then
Something went BUMP!
How that bump made us jump!
We looked!
Then we saw him step in on the mat!
We looked!
And we saw him!
The Cat in the Hat!
And he said to us,
"Why do you sit there like that?"

"I know it is wet
And the sun is not sunny.
But we can have
Lots of good fun that is funny!"

"I know some good games we could play."
Said the cat.
"I know some new tricks,"
Said the Cat in the Hat.
"A lot of good tricks.
I will show them to you.
Your mother
Will not mind at all if I do. . . ."

The Galloping Cat

STEVIE SMITH
(1902–1971)

Oh I am a cat that likes to
Gallop about doing good
So
One day when I was
Galloping about doing good, I saw
A Figure in the path; I said:
Get off! (Be-
cause
I am a cat that likes to
Gallop about doing good)
But he did not move, instead
He raised his hand as if
To land me a cuff
So I made to dodge so as to
Prevent him bringing it orf,
Un-for-tune-ately I slid
On a banana skin
Some Ass had left instead
Of putting in the bin. So
His hand caught me on the cheek
I tried
To lay his arm open from wrist to elbow
With my sharp teeth
Because I am
A cat that likes to gallop about doing good.

Would you believe it?
He wasn't there
My teeth met nothing but air,
But a Voice said: Poor cat,
(Meaning me) and a soft stroke
Came on me head
Since when
I have been bald
I regard myself as
A martyr to doing good.
Also I heard a swoosh
As of wings, and saw
A halo shining at the height of
Mrs Gubbins's backyard fence,
So I thought: What's the good
Of galloping about doing good
When angels stand in the path
And do not do as they should
Such as having an arm to be bitten off
All the same I
Intend to go on being
A cat that like to
Gallop about doing good
So
Now with my bald head I go,
Chopping the untidy flowers down, to
        and fro,
An' scooping up the grass to show
Underneath
The cinder path of wrath
Ha ha ha ha, ho.

Angels aren't the only ones who do
    not know
What's what and that
Galloping about doing good
Is a full-time job
That needs
An experienced eye of earthly
Sharpness, worth I dare say
(If you'll forgive a personal note)
A good deal more
Than all that skyey stuff
Of angels that make so bold as
To pity a cat like me that
Gallops about doing good.

From *the lives and times of archy and mehitabel*

DON MARQUIS
(1878–1937)

*Archy the cockroach and Mehitabel the cat first ap-
peared in the Sun Dial column of the New York Sun in
1916. The columns were laboriously written by Archy,
hopping from key to key, unable to hold down the shift
key. These two endearing and enduring animals created
by the columnist and poet Don Marquis continue to win
fans. Here are three poems concerning the adventures of
the romantic, dissolute feline Mehitabel.*

the song of mehitabel

this is the song of mehitabel
of mehitabel the alley cat
as i wrote you before boss
mehitabel is a believer
in the pythagorean
theory of the transmigration
of the soul and she claims
that formerly her spirit
was incarnated in the body
of cleopatra
that was a long time ago
and one must not be
surprised if mehitabel
has forgotten some of her
more regal manners

i have had my ups and downs
but wotthehell wotthehell
yesterday sceptres and crowns
fried oysters and velvet gowns
and today i herd with bums
but wotthehell wotthehell
i wake the world from sleep
as i caper and sing and leap
when i sing my wild free tune
wotthehell wotthehell
under the blear eyed moon
i am pelted with cast off shoon
but wotthehell wotthehell

do you think that i would change
my present freedom to range
for a castle or moated grange
wotthehell wotthehell
cage me and i d go frantic
my life is so romantic
capricious and corybantic
and i m toujours gai toujours gai

i know that i am bound
for a journey down the sound
in the midst of a refuse mound
but wotthehell wotthehell
oh i should worry and fret
death and i will coquette
there s a dance in the old dame yet
toujours gai toujours tai

i once was an innocent kit
wotthehell wotthehell
with a ribbon my neck to fit
and bells tied onto it
o wotthehell wotthehell
but a maltese cat came by
with a come hither look in his eye
and a song that soared to the sky
and wotthehell wotthehell
and i followed adown the street
the pad of his rhythmical feet
o permit me again to repeat
wotthehell wotthehell

my youth i shall never forget
but there s nothing i really regret
wotthehell wotthehell
there s a dance in the old dame yet
toujours gai toujours gai

the things that i had not ought to
i do because i ve gotto
wotthehell wotthehell
and i end with my favorite motto
toujours gai toujours gai

boss sometimes i think
that our friend mehitabel
is a trifle too gay

mehitabel tries
companionate marriage

boss i have seen mehitabel the cat
again and she has just been through
another matrimonial experience
she said in part as follows
i am always the sap archy
always the good natured simp
always believing in the good intentions
of those deceitful tom cats
always getting married at leisure
and repenting in haste
its wrong for an artist to marry
a free spirit has gotta
live her own life
about three months ago along came a
maltese tom with a black heart and
silver bells on his neck and says
mehitabel be mine
are you abducting me percy i asks him
so said he i am offering marriage
honorable up to date
companionate marriage
listen i said if its marriage
theres a catch in it somewheres
ive been married again and again
and its been my experience
that any kind of marriage
means just one dam kitten after another
and domesticity always ruins my art
but this companionate marriage says he
is all assets and no liabilities

its something new mehitabel
be mine mehitabel and i promise
a life of open ice boxes
creamed fish and catnip
well i said wotthehell kid
if its something new i will take a
chance theres a dance or two
in the old dame yet
i will try any kind of marriage once
you look like a gentleman to me percy
well archy i was wrong as usual
i wont go into details for i aint
any tabloid newspaper
but the way it worked out was i rustled
grub for that low lived bum for two
months and when the kittens came
he left me flat and he says these
offsprings dissolves the wedding
i am always the lady archy
i didn t do anything vulgar
i removed his left eye with one claw
and i says to him if i wasn t an
aristocrat id rip you
from gehenna to duodenum
the next four flusher that
says marriage to me
i may really lose my temper
trial marriage or companionate
marriage or old fashioned american
plan three meals a day marriage
with no thursdays off
they are all the same thing
marriage is marriage
and you cant laugh that curse off

                                        archy

no social stuff for mehitabel

i said to mehitabel
the cat i suppose you are
going to the swell cat
show i am not archy
said she i have as
much lineage as any
of those society
cats but i never could
see the conventional
social stuff archy
i am a lady
but i am bohemian
too archy i
live my own life
no bells and pink
ribbons for me
archy it is me for
the life romantic i could
walk right into
the cat show and get
away with it
archy none of those
maltese princesses has
anything on me in the
way of hauteur
or birth either or any
of the aristocratic
fixings and condiments
that mark the
cats of lady clara
vere de vere but
it bores me archy

me for the
wide open spaces the
alley serenade and
the moonlight
sonata on the back
fences i would
rather kill my own
rats and share
them with a
friend from greenwich
village than lap up
cream or beef juice
from a silver porringer
and have to
be polite to the
bourgeois clans
that feed me
wot the hell i
feel superior to that
stupid bunch me
for a dance
across the roofs when
the red star
calls to my blood
none of your
pretty puss stuff for
mehitabel it would
give me a grouch
to have to be so
solemn toujours
gai archy toujours
gai is my
motto

          archy

Homage to Octavian

JOSEPH ROCCASALVO
(b. 1940)

Who said cats have nine lives has told untruth.
For I once shared four lives with such a one
That bounded up the heights of feline youth
And, at the summit, shone so like the sun,
His angles were like angels. Yet undone
Was he, for though a cat of high estate,
He chose, in the fifth year of reign, to abdicate.

I wonder how Egypt, then, could bend its knee
And magnify his name as lord and liege,
And bow to all his elusive majesty,
Intoning words meant solely to besiege
That high-born soul to show noblesse oblige.
For he was to the godhead next of kin
Being, at all times, all he could have been.

But as for me, it was always otherwise;
I never knelt before his sinuous grace
Nor made obeisance to those lustrous eyes.
I lived too close to miracles to embrace
Him more than as a splendid commonplace.
And though he seemed to the gods their next of
    kin,
He proved to be mortally beautiful: Octavian.

From Dame Wiggins of Lee

Anonymous

Dame Wiggins of Lee
　　Was a worthy old soul
As e'er threaded a nee-
　　Dle or wash'd in a bowl;
She held mice and rats
　　In such antipathee
That seven fine cats
　　Kept Dame Wiggins of Lee.

The rats and mice scared
　　By this fierce-whiskered crew,
The poor seven cats
　　Soon had nothing to do;
So, as anyone idle
　　She ne'er loved to see;
She sent them to school,
　　Did Dame Wiggins of Lee.

But soon she grew tired
　　Of living alone;
So she sent for her cats
　　From school to come home,
Each rowing a wherry,
　　Returning you see;
The frolic made merry
　　Dame Wiggins of Lee.

The Dame was quite pleas'd
　　And ran out to market;
When she came back
　　They were mending the carpet.

91

The needle each handled
   As brisk as a bee.
"Well done, my good cats!"
   Said Dame Wiggins of Lee.

To give them a treat,
   She ran out for some rice;
When she came back they
   Were skating on ice.
"I shall soon see one down,
   Aye, perhaps two or three,
I'll bet half a crown,"
   Said Dame Wiggins of Lee.

They called the next day
   On the tomtit and sparrow,
And wheeled a poor sick lamb
   Home in a barrow.
"You shall all have some sprats
   For your humanitee,
My seven good cats,"
   Said Dame Wiggins of Lee.

While she ran to the field
   To look for its dam
They were warming the bed
   For the poor sick lamb:
They turned up the clothes
   All as neat as could be.
"I shall ne'er want a nurse,"
   Said Dame Wiggins of Lee.

She wished them good-night,
   And went up to bed;
When, lo! in the morning
   The cats were all fled.

But soon—what a fuss!
   "Where can they all be?
Here, pussy, puss, puss!"
   Cried Dame Wiggins of Lee.

The Dame's heart was nigh broke,
   So she sat down to weep,
When she saw them come back
   Each riding a sheep;
She fondled and patted
   Each purring Tommee:
"Ah! welcome, my dears,"
   Said Dame Wiggins of Lee.

The Dame was unable
   Her pleasure to smother
To see the sick lamb
   Jump up to its mother.
In spite of the gout
   And a pain in her knee,
She went dancing about,
   Did Dame Wiggins of Lee.

The farmer soon heard
   Where his sheep went astray,
And arrived at Dame's door
   With his faithful dog Tray.
He knocked with his crook,
   And the stranger to see,
Out of window did look
   Dame Wiggins of Lee.

For their kindness he had them
   All drawn by his team
And gave them some field mice
   And raspberry cream.

Said he, "All my stock
   You shall presently see,
For I *know* the cats
   Of Dame Wiggins of Lee."

The Cat and the
Two Sparrows

JEAN DE LA FONTAINE
(1621–1695)

To Milord the Duke of Burgundy

A Cat and a very young Sparrow, friends and peers,
Had lived side by side since earliest years.
Cage and basket shared household gods and laws.
The Bird's teasing the Cat produced no tears:
One fenced with his beak, the other one with his
   paws.
Cat always treated his friend with punctilio,
   Never failing to pull back his blow.
   His conscience would have had grave flaws
   Had his paw unsheathed its claws.
   Sparrow, behaving far less prudently,
   Pecked at him, hard and constantly.
   As a wise person using discretion,
   Master Cat excused this as play:

With friends one must never give into aggression
    When moved by wrath, on any day.
Since from infancy their friendship had so firmly
    stood,
Long habit kept them at peace, both day and night.
Never did play turn sour, or bring them to a fight,
    When a Sparrow from the neighborhood
Came to pay a visit, and then made a great show
Of amity for wise Raton and pert Pierrot,
The birds began to fight, with cries loud and shrill,
    And Raton then entered the fray.
"This stranger," he said, "comes here to mock us
    at will
    By insulting my friend this way!
This neighbor Sparrow's come to eat my brother!
No, by all cats!" Whereupon, plunging right into
    the spat,
He gobbled the intruder. "Really," observed Master
    Cat,
"Sparrows have exquisite, delicate flavor. Fancy
    that!"
This reflection likewise made him gobble up the
    other.

What moral can I now infer from this feat?
Without one every fable must remain incomplete.
I think I see, though very dimly, some features I
    may lose.
Prince, you'll at once have found those that fit:
The task is child's play for you, too hard for my
    Muse.
Neither she nor her Sisters have your store of wit.

Translated by Norman B. Spector

From Poor Matthias

MATTHEW ARNOLD
(1822–1888)

Here Arnold describes the cat Atossa.

Poor Matthias! Wouldst thou have
More than pity? claim'st a stave?
—Friends more near us than a bird
We dismiss'd without a word.
Rover, with the good brown head,
Great Atossa, they are dead;
Dead, and neither prose nor rhyme
Tells the praises of their prime.
Thou didst know them old and grey,
Know them in their sad decay.
Thou hast seen Atossa sage
Sit for hours beside thy cage;
Thou wouldst chirp, thou foolish bird,
Flutter, chirp—she never stirr'd!
What were now these toys to her?
Down she sank amid her fur;
Eyed thee with a soul resign'd—
And thou deemedst cats were kind!
—Cruel, but composed and bland,
Dumb, inscrutable and grand,
So Tiberius might have sat,
Had Tiberius been a cat.

From The Manciple's Tale

GEOFFREY CHAUCER
(C. 1340–1400)

Lat take a cat, and fostre him wel with milk
And tendre flessh[1], and make his couche of silk,
And lat hym seen a mous go by the wal,
Anon he weyveth[2] milk and flessh and al,
And every deyntee that is in that hous,
Swich[3] appetit hath he to ete a mous.
Lo, heere hath lust[4] his dominacioun,
And appetit fleemeth[5] discrecioun.

[1]meat
[2]abandons
[3]such
[4]desire, pleasure
[5]banishes

Chinese Proverb

ANONYMOUS

A lame cat
is bettter than a swift horse
when rats infest
the palace.

Verses on a Cat

PERCY BYSSHE SHELLEY
(1792–1822)

The poet composed these lines as a youth.

A cat in distress,
Nothing more, nor less;
Good folks, I must faithfully tell ye,
As I am a sinner,
It waits for some dinner
To stuff out its own little belly.

You would not easily guess
All the modes of distress
Which torture the tenants of earth;
And the various evils,
Which like so many devils,
Attend the poor souls from their birth.

Some a living require,
And others desire
An old fellow out of the way;
And which is the best
I leave to be guessed,
For I cannot pretend to say.

One wants society,
Another variety,
Others a tranquil life;
Some want food,
Others, as good,
Only want a wife.

But this poor little cat
Only wanted a rat,
To stuff out its own little maw;
And it were as good
Some people had such food,
To make them *hold their jaw!*

The Cat

OGDEN NASH
(1902–1971)

One gets a wife, one gets a house,
Eventually one gets a mouse.
One gets some words regarding mice,
One gets a kitty in a trice.
By two A.M., or thereabout,
The mouse is in, the cat is out.
It dawns upon one, in one's cot,
The mouse is still, the cat is not.
Instead of Pussy, says one's spouse,
One should have bought another mouse.

Country Cat

ELIZABETH COATSWORTH
(1893–1986)

"Where are you going, Mrs. Cat,
All by your lonesome lone?"
"Hunting a mouse, or maybe a rat
Where the ditches are overgrown."

"But you're very far from your house and home,
You've come a long, long way—"
"The further I wander, the longer I roam
The more I find mice at play."

"But you're very near to the dark pinewood
And foxes go hunting too."
"I know that a fox might find me good,
But what is a cat to do?

"I have my kittens who must be fed,
I *can't* have them skin and bone!"
And Mrs. Cat shook her brindled head
And went off by her lonesome lone.

Five Eyes

WALTER DE LA MARE
(1873–1956)

In Hans' old mill his three black cats
Watch his bins for the thieving rats.
Whisker and claw, they crouch in the night,
Their five eyes smouldering green and bright:
Squeaks from the flour sacks, squeaks from where
The cold wind stirs on the empty stair,
Squeaking and scampering, everywhere.
Then down they pounce, now in, now out,
At whisking tail, and sniffing snout;
While lean old Hans he snores away
Till peep of light at break of day;
Then up he climbs to his creaking mill,
Out come his cats all grey with meal—
Jekkel, and Jessup, and one-eyed Jill.

The Cat and an Old Rat

JEAN DE LA FONTAINE
(1621–1695)

In someone's book of fables I've read
That a second Nibblebacon, the Alexander of cats,
The Attila, the scourge of rats,
Filled them with misery, with dread.
I've read, I say, in a certain book, that
This cruel exterminator of a Cat,
A real Cerberus, held all for a league around in
fear.
His wish to rid the earth of all rodents was clear:
Planks suspended lightly so they'd crush their prey,
Ratsbane, every conceivable kind of snare,
Compared to him, were merely child's play.
So, once he'd become aware that, everywhere,
Mice were prisoners inside their lair,
Not daring to emerge, that in vain he then sought
their doom,
The rascal played dead, and from the ceiling in the
room
He let himself hang, head down. The wicked beast
Held on to ropes with a paw; the mouse folk at
least
Thought it was his punishment, imposed for
provocation;
That he'd stolen some roast or cheese from the
farm,
Scratched someone, caused a lot of damage, or
harm;
That they'd now hanged the rogue at this location.

All of them, I say, in high elation
Looked forward to great frolic at his inhumation.
They stuck their noses out, showed a little bit of
head.
Then each one went back inside his rat's nest,
Then took four steps outside, as a test.
Then, all went out to seek dinner, at last.
But they were guests at another repast:
The hanged villain revived and, dropping to his
feet,
Caught those who lagged behind.
"An old combat trick," he observed, gobbling his
treat.
"We know more than one. And all the deep holes
you'll find
Won't save you. I now inform you of the law:
You'll all descend into my maw."
Prophetic, our Master Cat, with cunning paw,
Once more tricked and lured them into his power.
He whitened his fur with some flour.
Thus disguised to Rat folk,
Crouched down, he tucked himself into an open
bin.
This was a real master stroke:
The quick-trotting nation came out, to lose their
skin.
One Rat, and no more, refrained from going to
sniff around.
He'd been to war and his knowledge of tricks was
profound.
In one battle, he'd even had to part with his tail.
"That block of flour sits down here to no avail!"
He shouted from far away so General Cat could
hear.

"Underneath I suspect I'll find some new device.
    Changing into flour won't suffice,
For even if you were an empty sack I'd not come
    near."
That was well said by him; I approve his prudence
    too.
    Experience gave him maturity,
    And wariness, as clearly he knew,
    Is the mother of maturity.

A Cat Came Fiddling
out of a Barn

ANONYMOUS
(TRADITIONAL)

A cat came fiddling out of a barn,
With a pair of bagpipes under her arm;
She could sing nothing but "Fiddle cum fee,
The mouse has married the bumble bee."
Pipe Cat, Dance Mouse;
We'll have a wedding at our good house.

A Fable of the Widow and Her Cat

JONATHAN SWIFT
(1667–1745)

A widow kept a favourite cat,
　　At first a gentle creature;
But when he was grown sleek and fat,
With many a mouse, and many a rat,
　　He soon disclosed his nature.

The fox and he were friends of old,
　　Nor could they now be parted;
They nightly slunk to rob the fold,
Devoured the lambs, the fleeces sold,
　　And puss grew lion-hearted.

He scratched her maid, he stole the cream,
　　He tore her best laced pinner;
Nor Chanticleer upon the beam,
Nor chick, nor duckling 'scapes, when Grim
　　Invites the fox to dinner.

The dame full wisely did decree,
　　For fear he should dispatch more,
That the false wretch should worried be:
But in a saucy manner he
　　Thus speeched it like a Lechmere.

'Must I, against all right and law,
　　Like pole-cat vile be treated?
I! who so long with tooth and claw
Have kept domestic mice in awe,
　　And foreign foes defeated!

'Your golden pippins, and your pies,
  How oft have I defended?
'Tis true, the pinner which you prize
I tore in frolic; to your eyes
  I never harm intended.

'I am a cat of honour—' 'Stay,'
  Quoth she, 'no longer parley;
Whate'er you did in battle slay,
By law of arms become your prey,
  I hope you won it fairly.

'Of this, we'll grant you stand acquit,
  But not of your outrages:
Tell me, perfidious! was it fit
To make my cream a *perquisite*,
  And steal to mend your wages?

'So flagrant is thy insolence,
  So vile thy breach of trust is;
That longer with thee to dispense,
Were want of power, or want of sense:
  Here, Towser!—Do him justice.'

Mother Tabbyskins

ELIZABETH ANNA HART
(1822–1888?)

Sitting at a window
In her cloak and hat,
I saw Mother Tabbyskins,
  The *real* old cat!
    Very old, very old,
    Crumplety and lame;
  Teaching kittens how to scold—
    Is it not a shame?

Kittens in the garden
Looking in her face,
Learning how to spit and swear—
  Oh, what a disgrace!
    Very wrong, very wrong,
    Very wrong and bad;
  Such a subject for our song,
    Makes us all too sad.

Old Mother Tabbyskins,
Sticking out her head,
Gave a howl, and then a yowl,
  Hobbled off to bed.
    Very sick, very sick,
    Very savage, too;
  Pray send for a doctor quick—
    Any one will do!

Doctor Mouse came creeping,
　　Creeping to her bed;
Lanced her gums and felt her pulse,
　　Whispered she was dead.
　　　　Very sly, very sly,
　　　　The *real* old cat
　　Open kept her weather eye—
　　　　Mouse! beware of that!

Old Mother Tabbyskins,
　　Saying 'Serves him right',
Gobbled up the doctor, with
　　Infinite delight.
　　　　Very fast, very fast
　　　　Very pleasant, too—
　　'What a pity it can't last!
　　　　Bring another, do!'

Doctor Dog comes running,
　　Just to see her begs;
Round his neck a comforter,
　　Trousers on his legs.
　　　　Very grand, very grand—
　　　　Golden-headed cane
　　Swinging gaily from his hand,
　　　　Mischief in his brain!

'Dear Mother Tabbyskins,
　　And how are you now?
Let me feel your pulse—so, so;
　　Show your tongue—bow, wow!
　　　　Very ill, very ill,
　　　　Please attempt to purr;
　　Will you take a draught or pill?
　　　　Which do you prefer?'

Ah, Mother Tabbyskins,
　　Who is now afraid?
Of poor little Doctor Mouse
　　You a mouthful made.
　　　　Very nice, very nice
　　　　Little doctor he;
　　But for Doctor Dog's advice
　　　　You must pay the fee.

Doctor Dog comes nearer,
　　Says she must be bled;
I heard Mother Tabbyskins
　　Screaming in her bed.
　　　　Very near, very near,
　　　　Scuffling out and in;
　　Doctor Dog looks full and queer—
　　　　Where is Tabbyskin?

I will tell the Moral
　　Without any fuss:
Those who lead the young astray
　　Always suffer thus.
　　　　Very nice, very nice,
　　　　Let our conduct be;
　　For all doctors are not mice,
　　　　Some are dogs, you see!

Two Little Kittens

ANONYMOUS
(C. 1879)

Two little kittens, one stormy night,
Began to quarrel, and then to fight;
One had a mouse, the other had none,
And that's the way the quarrel begun.

'I'll have that mouse,' said the biggest cat;
'You'll have that mouse? We'll see about that!'
'I *will* have that mouse,' said the eldest son;
'You *shan't* have the mouse,' said the little one.

I told you before 'twas a stormy night
When these two little kittens began to fight;
The old woman seized her sweeping broom,
And swept the two kittens right out of the room.

The ground was covered with frost and snow,
And the two little kittens had nowhere to go;
So they laid them down on the mat at the door,
While the old woman finished sweeping the floor.

Then they crept in, as quiet as mice,
All wet with the snow, and as cold as ice,
For they found it was better, that stormy night,
To lie down and sleep than to quarrel and fight.

The Cats of Kilkenny

ANONYMOUS
(TRADITIONAL)

There once were two cats of Kilkenny,
Each thought there was one cat too many;
So they fought and they fit,
And they scratched and they bit,
Till, excepting their nails
And the tips of their tails,
Instead of two cats, there weren't any.

The Three Little Kittens

ELIZA LEE FOLLEN
(1787–1860)

Three little kittens lost their mittens;
  And they began to cry,
    "Oh, mother dear,
    We very much fear
That we have lost our mittens."
    "Lost your mittens!
    You naughty kittens!
Then you shall have no pie!"
      "Mee-ow, mee-ow, mee-ow."
"No, you shall have no pie."
      "Mee-ow, mee-ow, mee-ow."

The three little kittens found their mittens;
  And they began to cry,
    "Oh, mother dear,
    See here, see here!
See, we have found our mittens!"
    "Put on your mittens,
    You silly kittens,
And you may have some pie."
      "Purr-r, purr-r, purr-r,
Oh, let us have the pie!
      Purr-r, purr-r, purr-r."

The three little kittens put on their mittens,
And soon ate up the pie;
"Oh, mother dear,
We greatly fear
That we have soiled our mittens!"
"Soiled your mittens!
You naughty kittens!"
Then they began to sigh,
"Mee-ow, mee-ow, mee-ow."
Then they began to sigh,
"Mee-ow, mee-ow, mee-ow."

The three little kittens washed their mittens,
And hung them out to dry,
"Oh, mother dear,
Do not you hear
That we have washed our mittens?"
"Washed your mittens!
Oh, you're good kittens!
But I smell a rat close by,
Hush, hush! Mee-ow, mee-ow."
"We smell a rat close by,
Mee-ow, mee-ow, mee-ow."

The Matron-Cat's Song

RUTH PITTER
(b. 1897)

So once again the trouble's o'er,
    And here I sit and sing;
Forgetful of my paramour
    And the pickle I was in:
Lord, lord, it is a trying time
    We bear when we're expecting,
When folk reproach us for the crime
    And frown with glance correcting.
So *purra wurra, purra wurra, pronkum pronkum*;
    Purra wurra, pronkum, pronkum purr.

How much I feared my kits would be
    Slain in the hour of birth!
And so I sought a sanctuary
    Which causes me some mirth;
The surly cook, who hates all cats,
    Hath here a little closet,
And here we nest among her hats—
    Lord save me when she knows it!
Hey purra wurra, etc.

Four kits have I of aspect fair,
    Though usually but three;
Two female tabs, a charming pair,
    Who much resemble me;
Lord, lord, to think upon the sport
    Which doth await the hussies;
They'll be no better than they ought,
    Nor worse than other pussies.
O purra wurra, etc.

Yet as becomes a mother fond
    I dote upon my boys,
And think they will excel beyond
    All other toms in noise;
How harsh their manly pelts will be,
    How stern and fixed each feature—
If they escape that cruelty
    Which man doth work on nature!
Ah *purra wurra*, etc.

Those eyes which now are sealèd fast
    Nine days against the light
Shall ere few months are overpast
    Like stars illume the night;
Those voices that with feeble squall
    Demand my whole attention,
Shall earn with rousing caterwaul
    Dishonourable mention.
Then *purra wurra*, etc.

But then, alas, I shall not care
    How flighty they may be,
For ere they're grown I'll have to bear
    Another four, or three;
And after all, they are the best
    While the whole crew reposes
With fast-shut eyes, weak limbs at rest,
    And little wrinkled noses.
So *purra wurra, purra wurra, pronkum pronkum:*
    Purra wurra pronkum, pronkum ryestraw;
Pronkum ryestraw, pronkum ryestraw,
    Pur-ra—wur-ra—pron-kum
Pronk . . . Foof.
               (She sleeps.)

Loulou and Her Cat

FREDERICK LOCKER-LAMPSON
(1821–1895)

Good pastry is vended
  In Cité Fadette;
Maison Pons can make splendid
  Brioche and *galette.*

M'sieu Pons is so fat that
  He's laid on the shelf;
Madame had a Cat that
  Was fat as herself.

Long hair, soft as satin,
  A musical purr,
'Gainst the window she'd flatten
  Her delicate fur

I drove Lou to see what
  Our neighbours were at,
In rapture, cried she, "What
  An exquisite cat!

"What whiskers! She's purring
  All over. Regale
Our eyes, *Puss*, by stirring
  Thy feathery tail!

"*M'sieu Pons*, will you sell her?"
  "*Ma femme est sortie,*
Your offer I'll tell her;
  But will she?" says he.

Yet *Pons* was persuaded
   To part with the prize:
(Our bargain was aided,
   My Lou, by your eyes!)

From his *légitime* save him—
   My spouse I prefer
For I warrant *his* gave him
   Un mauvais quart d'heure.

I am giving a pleasant
   Grimalkin to Lou,
—Ah, *Puss*, what a present
   I'm giving to you!

As I Was Going to St. Ives

ANONYMOUS
(TRADITIONAL)

As I was going to St. Ives,
I met a man with seven wives,
Each wife had seven sacks,
Each sack had seven cats,
Each cat had seven kits:
Kits, cats, sacks, and wives,
How many were there going to St. Ives?

The Cat Metamorphosed into a Woman

JEAN DE LA FONTAINE
(1621–1695)

A Man loved his Cat with a love quite fanatic;
He thought her darling, lovely, dainty, and
    dramatic.
    Her little meouw, sweet and sad,
    Drove him madder than the mad.
  This man, then, through tears and prayer,
    Magic, spells cast everywhere,
    Tried so hard that Fate gave way
    And made his Cat, one fine day,
    A woman. At once, before noon,
    Master fool tied the wedding knot.
    Mad love now marked his honeymoon
    Where once fond folly was his lot.
    Never did fair lady's charms
    So bewitch her suitor at all
    As completely as this new wife's arms
    Held her mad spouse in thrall.
    He coddled her, she made him purr.
    He saw no further trace of cat in her
    And, permitting error to run unchecked,
    Was finding her woman in every respect,
When some mice, gnawing away at the mat where
    they were,
Interrupted the joy of this pair just newly wed.
    At once the wife sprang from her bed.

"Her leap did not strike true.
Back came mice to wife crouched in their view,
  And this time her pounce was just right.
    For, since her form was new,
    On seeing her the mice felt no fright.
    Lured to them she was at any hour,
    Such is inner nature's power.
It scoffs at everything, once the years have taken
  hold.
The vase is saturated, set; the cloth has seized its
  fold.
    In vain from its accustomed course
    One tries to make it swerve.
    No matter what one does to force
    It, no reform will serve.
    Blows of pitchfork or of scourge
    Cannot transform the basic urge.
    Armed with stick, or mace,
  You'll never bring it to its knees.
Close the door right in its face,
Through windows it returns with ease.

Translated by Norman B. Spector

The Cat

CHARLES BAUDELAIRE
(1821–1867)

Come, my fine cat, against my loving heart;
Sheathe your sharp claws, and settle.
And let my eyes into your pupils dart
Where agate sparks with metal.

Now while my fingertips caress at leisure
Your head and wiry curves,
And that my hand's elated with the pleasure
Of your electric nerves,

I think about my woman—how her glances
Like yours, dear beast, deep-down
And cold, can cut and wound one as with lances;

Then, too, she has that vagrant
And subtle air of danger that makes fragrant
Her body, lithe and brown.

Translated by Roy Campbell

My cat and i

ROGER MCGOUGH
(b. 1937)

Girls are simply the prettiest things
My cat and i believe
And we're always saddened
When it's time for them to leave

We watch them titivating
(that often takes a while)
And though they keep us waiting
My cat & i just smile

We like to see them to the door
Say how sad it couldn't last
Then my cat and I go back inside
And talk about the past.

The White Cat of Trenarren

A. L. ROWSE
(b. 1903)

(for Beryl Cloke)

He was a mighty hunter in his youth
At Polmear all day on the mound, on the pounce
For anything moving, rabbit or bird or mouse—
    My cat and I grow old together.

After a day's hunting he'd come into the house
Delicate ears stuck all with fleas.
At Trenarren I've heard him sigh with pleasure
After a summer's day in the long-grown leas—
    My cat and I grow old together.

When I was a child I played all day,
With only a little cat for companion,
At solitary games of my own invention
Under the table or up in the green bay—
    My cat and I grow old together.

When I was a boy I wandered the roads
Up to the downs by gaunt Carn Grey,
Wrapt in a dream at the end of day,
All round me the moor, below me the bay—
    My cat and I grow old together.

Now we are too often apart, yet
Turning out of Central Park into the Plaza,
Or walking Michigan Avenue against the lake-wind,
I see a little white shade in the shrubbery
Of far-off Trenarren, never far from my mind—
    My cat and I grow old together.

When I come home from too much travelling,
Cautiously he comes out of his lair to my call,
Receives me at first with a shy reproach
At long absence to him incomprehensible—
    My cat and I grow old together.

Incapable of much or long resentment,
He scratches at my door to be let out
In early morning in the ash moonlight,
Or red dawn breaking through Mother Bond's
    spinney—
    My cat and I grow old together.

No more frisking as of old,
Or chasing his shadow over the lawn,
But a dignified old person, tickling
His nose against twig or flower in the border,
Until evening falls and bed-time's in order,
Unable to keep eyes open any longer
He waits for me to carry him upstairs
To nestle all night snug at foot of bed—
    My cat and I grow old together.

Careful of his licked and polished appearance,
Ears like shell-whorls pink and transparent,
White plume waving proudly over the paths,
Against a background of sea and blue hydrangeas—
    My cat and I grow old together.

On the Death of a Cat, a Friend of Mine Aged Ten Years and a Half

CHRISTINA ROSSETTI
(1830–1894)

Who shall tell the lady's grief
When her cat was past relief?
Who shall number the hot tears
Shed o'er her, belov'd for years?
Who shall say the dark dismay
Which her dying caused that day?

Come ye Muses, one and all,
Come obedient to my call;
Come and mourn with tuneful breath
Each one for a separate death;
And, while you in numbers sigh,
I will sing her elegy.

Of a noble race she came,
And Grimalkin was her name.
Young and old full many a mouse
Felt the prowess of her house;
Weak and strong full many a rat
Cowered beneath her crushing pat;
And the birds around the place
Shrank from her too-close embrace.
But one night, reft of her strength,
She lay down and died at length:
Lay a kitten by her side
In whose life the mother died.

Spare her life and lineage,
Guard her kitten's tender age,
And that kitten's name as wide
Shall be known as hers that died.
And whoever passes by
The poor grave where Puss doth lie,
Softly, softly let him tread,
Nor disturb her narrow bed.

My Old Cat

HAL SUMMERS
(b. 1911)

My old cat is dead,
Who would butt me with his head.
He had the sleekest fur.
He had the blackest purr.
Always gentle with us
Was this black puss,
But when I found him today
Stiff and cold where he lay
His look was a lion's,
Full of rage, defiance:
Oh, he would not pretend
That what came was a friend
But met it in pure hate.
Well died, my old cat.

A Favourite Cat's Dying Soliloquy, Addressed to Mrs. Patton of Lichfield

ANNA SEWARD
(1747–1809)

Long years beheld me PATTON'S mansion grace,
The gentlest, fondest of the feline race;
Before her frisking thro' the garden glade,
Or at her feet, in quiet slumber, laid;
Prais'd for my glossy back, of tortoise streak,
And the warm smoothness of my snowy neck;
Soft paws, that sheath'd for her the clawing nail;
The shining whisker, and meand'ring tail.
Now feeble age each glazing eye-ball dims;
And pain has stiffen'd these once supple limbs;
Fate of eight lives the forfeit gasp obtains,
And e'en the ninth creeps languid thro' my veins.

Much, sure, of good the future has in store,
When Lucy basks on PATTON'S hearth no more,
In those blest climes where fishes oft forsake
The winding river and the glassy lake;
There as our silent-footed race behold
The spots of crimson and the fins of gold,
Venturing beyond the shielding waves to stray,
They gasp on shelving banks, our easy prey;
While birds unwing'd hop careless o'er the ground,
And the plump mouse incessant trots around,
Near wells of cream, which mortals never skim,
Warm marum creeping round their shallow brim;

Where green valerian tufts, luxuriant spread,
Cleanse the sleek hide, and form the fragrant bed.

Yet, stern dispenser of the final blow,
Before thou lay'st an aged Grimalkin low,
Bend to her last request a gracious ear,
Some days, some few short days to linger here!
So, to the guardian of her earthly weal
Shall softest purs these tender truths reveal:
Ne'er shall thy now expiring Puss forget
To thy kind cares her long-enduring debt;
Nor shall the joys that painless realms decree,
Efface the comforts once bestow'd by thee;
To countless mice thy chicken bones preferr'd,
Thy toast to golden fish and wingless bird:
O'er marum border and valerian bed
Thy Lucy shall decline her moping head;
Sigh that she climbs no more, with grateful glee,
Thy downy sofa and thy cradling knee;
Nay, e'en by wells of cream shall sullen swear,
Since PATTON, her lov'd mistress, is not there.

Warm marum: The affection of cats for marum and valerian
is well known. They will beat down the stems, mat them
with their feet, and roll upon them. (Note from Sir Walter
Scott's edition of 1810.)

Upon a Friend's Pet Cat, Being Sick

JOHN WINSTANLEY
(1678–1751)

How fickle's Health! when sickness thus
So sharp, so sudden visits *Puss!*
A warning fair, and Instance good,
To show how frail are Flesh and Blood,
That Fate has Mortals at a Call,
Men, Women, Children—Cats and all.
Nor should we fear, despair, or sorrow,
If well to-day, and ill to-morrow,
Grief being but a Med'cine vain,
For griping Gut, or asking Brain,
And Patience the best Cure for Pain.
How brisk and well, last Week, was *Puss!*
How sleek, and plump, as one of us:
Yet now, alack! and well-a-day!
How dull, how rough, and fall'n away.
How feintly creeps about the House!
Regardless or of Play, or Mouse;
Nor stomach has, to drink, or eat,
Of sweetest Milk, or daintiest Meat;
A grievious this, and sore Disaster
To all the House, but most his Master,
Who sadly takes it thus to heart,
As in his Pains he bore a part.
And, what increases yet his Grief,
Is, nought can cure, or give Relief,
No Doctor caring to prescribe,
Or Med'cine give, for Love, or Bribe,

Nor other Course, but to petition
Dame Nature, oft the best Physician,
The readiest too, and cheapest sure,
Since she ne'er asks a Fee for Cure
Nor ever takes a single Shilling,
As many basely do for killing.
So, for a while, snug let him lye,
As Fates decree, to live or dye,
While I, in dismal dogrel Verse,
His Beauties and his Fame rehearse.
Poor *Bob!* how have I smiled to see
Thee sitting on thy Master's Knee?
While, pleased to stroke thy Tabby-coat,
Sweet Purrings warbling in thy Throat,
He would with rapturous Hug declare,
No Voice more sweet, or Maid more fair.
No Prating Poll, or Monkey bold,
Was more caress'd by Woman old,
Nor flutt'ring Fop, with Am'rous Tongue,
So much admir'd by Virgin Young.
Miss *Betty*'s Bed-fellow, and Pet,
(Too young to have another yet),
At Dinner, he'd beside her sit,
Fed from her Mouth with sweetest Bit;
Not Mrs L——'s so charming *Philly*
Was more familiar, fond, or silly,
Nor Mrs C——'s ugly Cur
Made more a foustre, or more stir.
Oft tir'd and cloy'd, with being petted,
Or else by *Molly* beaten, fretted,
He'd out into the Garden run,
To sleep in th' Shade, or bask in th' Sun;
Sometimes about the Walks he'd ramble,
Or on the verdant Green would amble,

Or under the hedges sculking sit,
To catch the unwary *Wren*, or *Tit*,
Or *Sparrows* young, which Sun-beams hot
Had forc'd to quit their mansion Pot,
Then murther with relentless Claws.
Now, cruel Death, so fierce and grim,
With gaping jaws does threaten him,
While pining, he, with Sickness sore,
Oppress'd and griev'd, can hunt no more.

Now joyful Mice skip, frisk, and play,
And safely revel, Night and Day.
The Garrets, Kitchens, Stairs, and Entry,
Unguarded by that Dreadful Centry.

The Pantry now is open set,
No fear for *Puss* therein to get,
With Chicken cold to run away,
Or sip the Cream set by for Tea;
Jenny now need not watch the Door,
Or for lost Meat repine no more,
Nor *Molly* many a scolding dread
For slamming him from off the Bed;
Poor harmless Animal! now lies
As who can say, he lives or dies.
Tho' I have heard a saying that
Some three times three Lives has a Cat;
Should Death then now the Conquest gain,
And feeble *Bob*, with struggle vain,
To his resistless Fate give way,
Yet come to Life, another Day,
How will Time scratch his old bald Pate,
To see himself so *Bobb'd*, so Bit,

To find that *Bob* has eight Lives more
To lose, e'er he can him secure.
Should he however, his Bout dye,
What Pen should write his Elegy?
No living Bard is fit, not One;
Since *Addison*, and Parnel's gone;
Or such another Pen, as that
Which wrote so fine on Mountaign's Cat.

That Little Black Cat

D'ARCY WENTWORTH THOMPSON
(1829–1902)

Who's that ringing at our door-bell?
  'I'm a little black cat, and I'm not very well.'
'Then rub your little nose with a little mutton-fat,
  And that's the best cure for a little pussy cat.'

A Dirge for a Righteous Kitten

VACHEL LINDSAY
(1879–1931)

(To be intoned, all but the two italicized lines, which are to be spoken in a snappy, matter-of-fact way)

Ding-dong, ding-dong, ding-dong.
Here lies a kitten good, who kept
A kitten's proper place.
He stole no pantry eatables,
Nor scratched the baby's face.
He let the alley-cats alone.
He had no yowling vice.
His shirt was always laundried well,
He freed the house of mice.
Until his death he had not caused
His little mistress tears,
He wore his ribbon prettily,
He washed behind his ears.
Ding-dong, ding-dong, ding-dong.

The Golden Cat

ELEANOR FARJEON
(1881–1965)

My golden cat has dappled sides;
No prince has worn so fine a cloak,
Patterned like sea-water where rides
The sun, or like the flower in oak
When the rough plank has been planed out,
Lovely as yellow mackerel skies
In moonlight, or a speckled trout.
Clear as swung honey were his eyes.

It was a wondrous daily thing
To look for, when his beautiful
Curved body gathered for a spring
That, light as any golden gull,
Flashed over the fine net of wire
Which my casement-window bars;
His leap was bright as tongues of fire,
And swift as autumn shooting-stars.

My cat was like a golden gift,
A golden myth of Grecian lore—
But things so bright, and things so swift,
Must vanish; and he is no more.

Ode on the Death of a Favorite Cat, Drowned in a Tub of Gold Fishes

Thomas Gray
(1716–1771)

'Twas on a lofty vase's side,
Where China's gayest art had dy'd
  The azure flowers, that blow;
Demurest of the tabby kind,
The pensive Selima reclin'd,
  Gazed on the lake below.

Her conscious tail her joy declar'd;
The fair round face, the snowy beard,
  The velvet of her paws,
Her coat, that with the tortoise vies,
Her ears of jet, and emerald eyes,
  She saw; and purr'd applause.

Still had she gaz'd; but 'midst the tide
Two angel forms were seen to glide,
  The Genii of the stream:
Their scaly armour's Tyrian hue
Thro' richest purple to the view
  Betray'd a golden gleam.

The hapless Nymph with wonder saw:
A whisker first and then a claw,
   With many an ardent wish,
She stretch'd in vain to reach the prize.
What female heart can gold despise?
   What Cat's averse to fish?

Presumptuous Maid! with looks intent
Again she stretch'd, again she bent,
   Nor knew the gulf between.
(Malignant Fate sat by, and smil'd)
The slipp'ry verge her feet beguil'd,
   She tumbled headlong in.

Eight times emerging from the flood
She mew'd to ev'ry watry God,
   Some speedy aid to send.
No Dolphin came, no Nereid stirr'd:
Nor cruel *Tom*, nor *Susan* heard.
   A Fav'rite has no friend!

From hence, ye Beauties, undeceiv'd,
Know, one false step is ne'er retriev'd,
   And be with caution bold.
Not all that tempts your wand'ring eyes
And heedless hearts, is lawful prize;
   Nor all, that glisters, gold.

Last Words to a Dumb Friend

Thomas Hardy
(1840–1928)

Pet was never mourned as you,
Purrer of the spotless hue,
Plumy tail, and wistful gaze
While you humoured our queer ways,
Or outshrilled your morning call
Up the stairs and through the hall—
Foot suspended in its fall—
While, expectant, you would stand
Arched, to meet the stroking hand;
Till your way you chose to wend
Yonder, to your tragic end.

Never another pet for me!
Let your place all vacant be;
Better blankness day by day
Than companion torn away.
Better bid his memory fade,
Better blot each mark he made,
Selfishly escape distress
By contrived forgetfulness,
Than preserve his prints to make
Every mom and eve an ache.

From the chair whereon he sat
Sweep his fur, nor wince thereat;
Rake his little pathways out
Mid the bushes roundabout;
Smooth away his talons' mark
From the claw-worn pine-tree bark,

Where he climbed as dusk
    embrowned,
Waiting us who loitered round.

Strange it is this speechless thing,
Subject to our mastering,
Subject for his life and food
To our gift, and time, and mood;
Timid pensioner of us Powers,
His existence ruled by ours,
Should—by crossing at a breath
Into save and shielded death,
By the merely taking hence
Of his insignificance—
Loom as largened to the sense,
Shape as part, above man's will,
Of the Imperturbable.

As a prisoner, flight debarred,
Exercising in a yard,
Still retain I, troubled, shaken,
Mean estate, by him forsaken;
And this home, which scarcely took
Impress from his little look,
By his faring to the Dim
Grows all eloquent of him.

Housemate, I can think you still
Bounding to the window-sill,
Over which I vaguely see
Your small mound beneath the tree,
Showing in the autumn shade
That you moulder where you played.

2 October 1904

137

To a Cat

Algernon Charles Swinburne
(1837–1909)

I

Stately, kindly, lordly friend,
  Condescend
Here to sit by me, and turn
Glorious eyes that smile and burn,
Golden eyes, love's lustrous meed,
On the golden page I read.

All your wondrous wealth of hair,
  Dark and fair,
Silken-shaggy, soft and bright
As the clouds and beams of night,
Pays my reverent hand's caress
Back with friendlier gentleness.

Dogs may fawn on all and some
  As they come;
You, a friend of loftier mind,
Answer friends alone in kind.
Just your foot upon my hand
Softly bids it understand.

Morning round this silent sweet
    Garden-seat
Sheds its wealth of gathering light,
Thrills the gradual clouds with might,
Changes woodland, orchard, heath,
Lawn, and garden there beneath.

Fair and dim they gleamed below:
    Now they glow
Deep as even your sunbright eyes,
Fair as even the wakening skies.
Can it not or can it be
Now that you give thanks to see?

May you not rejoice as I,
    Seeing the sky
Change to heaven revealed, and bid
Earth reveal the heaven it hid
All night long from stars and moon,
Now the sun sets all in tune?

That within you wakes with day
    Who can say?
All to little may we tell,
Friends who like each other well,
What might haply, if we might,
Bid us read our lives aright.

II

Wild on woodland ways your sires
    Flashed like fires;
Fair as flame and fierce and fleet
As with wings on wingless feet
Shone and sprang your mother, free,
Bright and brave as wind or sea.

Free and proud and glad as they,
    Here to-day
Rests or roams their radiant child,
Vanquished not, but reconciled,
Free from curb of aught above
Save the lovely curb of love.

Love through dreams of souls divine
    Fain would shine
Round a dawn whose light and song
Then should right our mutual wrong—
Speak, and seal the love-lit law
Sweet Assisi's seer foresaw.

Dreams were theirs; yet haply may
    Dawn a day
When such friends and fellows born,
Seeing our earth as fair at morn,
May for wiser love's sake see
More of heaven's deep heart than we.

The Tiger

WILLIAM BLAKE
(1757–1827)

Tiger! Tiger! burning bright
In the forests of the night
What immortal hand or eye
Could frame thy fearful symmetry?

In what distant deeps or skies
Burned the fire of thine eyes?
On what wings dare he aspire?
What the hand dare seize the fire?

And what shoulder, and what art,
Could twist the sinews of thy heart?
And when thy heart began to beat,
What dread hand? And what dread feet?

What the hammer? What the chain?
In what furnace was thy brain?
What the anvil? What dread grasp
Dare its deadly terrors clasp?

When the stars threw down their
    spears,
And watered heaven with their tears,
Did he smile his work to see?
Did he who made the Lamb make thee?

Tiger! Tiger! burning bright
In the forests of the night,
What immortal hand or eye
Dare frame thy fearful symmetry?

Divination by a Cat

ANTHONY HECHT
(b. 1923)

Fence walker, balancer, your devil-may-care
Astounds the workman teetering on his girder
Whom gravity and the pavement want to murder,
    But with eight lives to spare
Who would lack courage? From his jungle-gym
He lowers, thin as a hair, the strand of fear
To plumb the seventy stories under him,
    And for his firm intent
The spirit level of the inner ear
    Is his chief instrument.

But you are classic, striking the S-curve
In a half-gainer from some eminence,
And with Athenian equipoise and sense
    To qualify your nerve,
End up unerringly upon your feet.
O this is Greek to all of us. I dare
Construe your figure for our human fate,
    And like the Pythoness
Decoding viscera, anoint the air
    With emblematic guess.

You are the lesser Tiger, yet the night
Blazes with the combustion of your eye,
And we, in our imperfect symmetry,
   Combining double sight,
Can see mirrored in your chatoyant gaze
Our fire, slight, diminished. If the first
Intensity return of that white blaze
   To run our bodies through,
Might it not burn us? If the fire burst,
   Will it not barbecue?

Cat, you are meat for study. All our youth
Shall vanish, like your literary kin,
Dwindle into a disembodied grin;
   And if we want the truth,
Why, we must cram for it, gather your drift,
Like that odd family trudging from St. Ives.
Be Plutarch to our ignorance; your gift
   Compares Athens to Rome,
And the collected tails of all your lives
   Shall drive the moral home.

Cats

CHARLES BAUDELAIRE
(1821–1867)

Sages austere and fervent lovers both,
In their ripe season, cherish cats, the pride
Of hearths, strong, mild, and to themselves allied
In chilly stealth and sedentary sloth.

Friends both to lust and learning, they frequent
Silence, and love the horror darkness breeds.
Erebus would have chosen them for steeds
To hearses, could their pride to it have bent.

Dreaming, the noble postures they assume
Of sphinxes stretching out into the gloom
That seems to swoon into an endless trance.

Their fertile flanks are full of sparks that tingle,
And particles of gold, like grains of shingle,
Vaguely be-star their pupils as they glance.

Translated by Roy Campbell

From *Jubilate Agno*

CHRISTOPHER SMART
(1722–1771)

For I will consider my Cat Jeoffry.

For his is the servant of the Living God duly and daily serving him.

For at the first glance of the glory of God in the East he worships in his way.

For is this done by wreathing his body seven times round with elegant quickness.

For then he leaps up to catch the musk, wch is the blessing of God upon his prayer.

For he rolls upon prank to work it in.

For having done duty and received blessing he begins to consider himself.

For this he performs in ten degrees.

For first he looks upon his fore-paws to see if they are clean.

For secondly he kicks up behind to clear away there.

For thirdly he works it upon stretch with the fore-paws extended.

For fourthly he sharpens his paws by wood.

For fifthly he washes himself.

For Sixthly he rolls upon wash.

For Seventhly he fleas himself, that he may not be interrupted upon the beat.

For Eighthly he rubs himself against a post.

For Ninthly he looks up for his instructions.

For Tenthly he goes in quest of food.

For having consider'd God and himself he will consider his neighbour.

For if he meets another cat he will kiss her in
kindness.

For when he takes his prey he plays with it to give
it a chance.

For one mouse in seven escapes by his dallying.

For when his day's work is done his business more
properly begins.

For he keeps the Lord's watch in the night against
the adversary.

For he counteracts the powers of darkness by his
electrical skin & glaring eyes.

For he counteracts the Devil, who is death, by
brisking about the life.

For in his morning orisons he loves the sun and
the sun loves him.

For his is of the tribe of Tiger.

For the Cherub Cat is a term of the Angel Tiger.

For he has the subtlety and hissing of a serpent,
which in goodness he suppresses.

For he will not do destruction, if he is well-fed,
neither will he spit without provocation.

For he purrs in thankfulness, when God tells him
he's a good Cat.

For he is an instrument for the children to learn
benevolence upon.

For every house is incompleat without him & a
blessing is lacking in the spirit.

For the Lord commanded Moses concerning the
cats at the departure of the Children of Israel
from Egypt.

For every family had one cat at least in the bag.

For the English Cats are the best in Europe.

For he is the cleanest in the use of his fore-paws
of any quadrupede.

For the dexterity of his defence is an instance of
the love of God to him exceedingly.

For he is the quickest to his mark of any creature.

For he is tenacious of his point.

For he is a mixture of gravity and waggery.

For he knows that God is his Saviour.

For there is nothing sweeter than his peace when
at rest.

For there is nothing brisker than his life when in
motion.

For he is of the Lord's poor and so indeed is he
called by benevolence perpetually—Poor
Jeoffry! poor Jeoffry! the rat has bit thy
throat.

For I bless the name of the Lord Jesus that Jeoffry
is better.

For the divine spirit comes about his body to
sustain it in compleat cat.

For his tongue is exceeding pure so that it has in
purity what it wants in musick.

For he is docile and can learn certain things.

For he can set up with gravity which is patience
upon approbation.

For he can fetch and carry, which is patience in
employment.

For he can jump over a stick which is patience
upon proof positive.

For he can spraggle upon waggle at the word of
command.

For he can jump from an eminence into his
master's bosom.

For he can catch the cork and toss it again.

For he is hated by the hypocrite and miser.

For the former is afraid of detection.

For the latter refuses the charge.

For he camels his back to bear the first notion of business.

For he is good to think on, if a man would express himself neatly.

For he made a great figure in Egypt for his signal services.

For he killed the Icneumon-rat very pernicious by land.

For his ears are so acute that they sting again.

For from this proceeds the passing quickness of his attention.

For by stroking of him I have found out electricity.

For I perceived God's light about him both wax and fire.

For the Electrical fire is the spiritual substance, which God sends from heaven to sustain the bodies both of man and beast.

For God has blessed him in the variety of his movements.

For, tho he cannot fly, he is an excellent clamberer.

For his motions upon the face of the earth are more than any other quadrupede.

For he can tread to all the measures upon the musick.

For he can swim for life.

For he can creep.

The Cat of Cats

WILLIAM BRIGHTY RANDS
(1823–1882)

I am the cat of cats. I am
   The everlasting cat!
Cunning, and old, and sleek as jam,
   The everlasting cat!
I hunt the vermin in the night—
   The everlasting cat!
For I see best without the light—
   The everlasting cat!

Index of Titles

Index of
Authors and Translators